Along the Hudson

Along the Hudson
Walking Manhattan's Western Waterfront

WILLIAM J. HENNESSEY

excelsior editions
State University of New York Press
Albany, New York

Cover photo: The Little Red Lighthouse. Photo by the author.

Unless otherwise noted, all photographs are by the author.
All maps created by Map Hero.

Published by State University of New York Press, Albany

© 2025 State University of New York

All rights reserved

Printed in the United States of America

No part of this book may be used or reproduced in any manner whatsoever without written permission. No part of this book may be stored in a retrieval system or transmitted in any form or by any means including electronic, electrostatic, magnetic tape, mechanical, photocopying, recording, or otherwise without the prior permission in writing of the publisher.

Links to third-party websites are provided as a convenience and for informational purposes only. They do not constitute an endorsement or an approval of any of the products, services, or opinions of the organization, companies, or individuals. SUNY Press bears no responsibility for the accuracy, legality, or content of a URL, the external website, or for that of subsequent websites.

EU GPSR Authorised Representative:
Logos Europe, 9 rue Nicolas Poussin, 17000, La Rochelle, France
contact@logoseurope.eu

Excelsior Editions is an imprint of State University of New York Press

For information, contact State University of New York Press, Albany, NY
www.sunypress.edu

Library of Congress Cataloging-in-Publication Data

Name: Hennessey, William J. (William John), author.
Title: Along the Hudson : walking Manhattan's western waterfront / William J. Hennessey.
Identifiers: LCCN 2024049454 | ISBN 9798855802856 (pbk. : alk. paper) | ISBN 9798855802863 (ebook)
Subjects: LCSH: Manhattan (New York, N.Y.)—Tours. | Walking—New York (State)—New York—Guidebooks. | Waterfronts—New York (State)—New York—Guidebooks. | Manhattan (New York, N.Y.)—Buildings, structures, etc.—Guidebooks | Manhattan (New York, N.Y.)—Description and travel.
Classification: LCC F128.18 .H397 2025 | DDC 917.47/10444—dc23/eng/20250203
LC record available at https://lccn.loc.gov/2024049454

Contents

Preface	vii
Acknowledgments	ix
The Hudson—Some Historical Background	xi
1. The Battery	1
2. Battery Park City	19
3. Chambers Street to Gansevoort Street	45
4. Gansevoort Street to the Javits Center	67
5. The Javits Center to 72nd Street	87
6. 72nd Street to 110th Street	103
7. 110th Street to 153rd Street	129
8. 153rd Street to Spuyten Duyvil	149
Bibliography	169

Preface

During my junior year in high school, I had a summer job on Wall Street. Every morning, I would join the suit-and-tie-clad, newspaper-toting commuters on the Erie Lackawanna, taking my place in the rickety old railway cars that daily carried thousands from suburban New Jersey to Hoboken Terminal on the western bank of the Hudson. Many of my fellow passengers, eager to get to their offices quickly, opted for a PATH train across the river, but I always made sure that I allowed enough time to take one of the old steam ferries that plied between Hoboken and Barclay Street. The 15-minute journey was the highlight of my day. I clung to the rail, scanning the river for whatever passenger liners were in port, watching the tugs at work, and hoping for a passing fireboat. Mostly, however, I stared at the Oz-like skyline rising majestically above the river. For me the view was truly magical. That magic evaporated quickly, however, once the boat reached Manhattan. This was the mid-1960s, and on both sides of the ferry terminal decay and neglect were everywhere. The once vital waterfront was on life support, and a depressing gray barrier of abandoned wharfs divided the still-bustling and glamorous city from the river that had long been its life blood.

Returning to the city now after many years away, the Hudson is once again a part of my daily life. From my breakfast table I can survey the river, consider the state of the Palisades, and check on traffic moving over the George Washington Bridge. I never tire of looking at the barges, sailboats, and sight-seeing boats passing by. My view was an invitation to explore the river more closely. I began walking along its banks and was astonished by how much things have changed. Over the past half a century the city's Hudson waterfront has been transformed from a rotting wasteland into a walker's paradise. The old wharfs, piers, and warehouses that for so long separated New Yorkers from their river have been swept away, replaced by a handsome sequence of parks and riverside promenades. I was fascinated and excited by the transformation, and this book is a direct response to what I have seen and experienced strolling and photographing along Manhattan's revitalized 13-mile western shoreline.

Through eight riverside walks we will "cover the waterfront" as it looks today, exploring its history, architecture, and ecology, occasionally gazing across the river to the opposite shore. As we walk, we will consider notable buildings, parks, and civic spaces along the way, as well as the infrastructure lying under the river and some of the objects floating on its surface. Above all, the book's goal is to provide a framework through which walkers can discover for themselves the history, beauty, energy, and fascination of a great river and its relationship to a great city.

Figure I.1. Map showing each of the walking tours covered in the book.

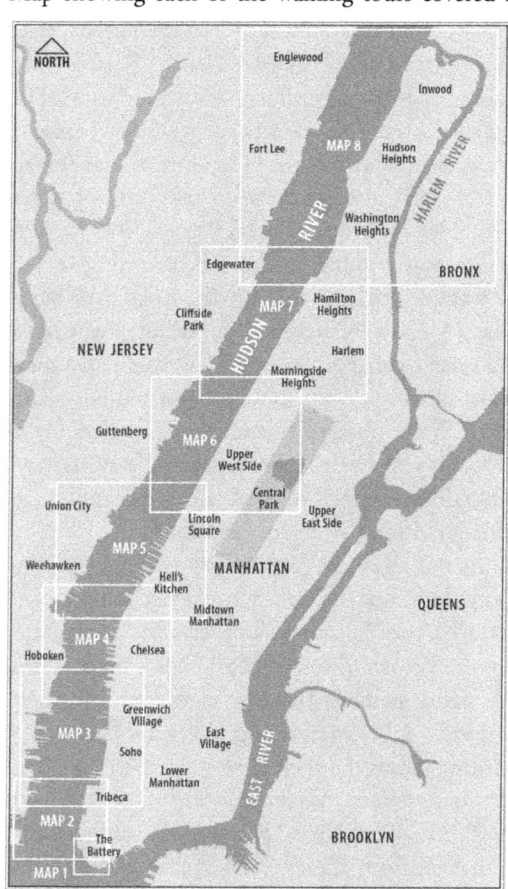

Acknowledgments

Books like this are team efforts. Throughout, I've relied heavily on the work of other authors and researchers and am deeply in their debt. I've also benefited greatly from the support and encouragement of friends and colleagues.

Matt Kania of Map Hero, Kenneth Cobb at the New York City Municipal Archives, and Nicholas Sbordone at the Battery Park City Authority have been particularly helpful, as have the staffs of the Milstein Division and Art and Architecture Collections of the New York Public Library. At SUNY Press, my editor, Richard Carlin, and his colleagues have been as thoughtful and encouraging as they are professional.

Finally, my family, especially my wife Leslie Griffin Hennessey, have been unstinting in their enthusiasm, patience, and editorial support. Without them, this book would not have happened.

The Hudson—Some Historical Background

The North American continent is crisscrossed by many justly famous rivers—the Mississippi, Missouri, Ohio, Rio Grande, Colorado, and Columbia. Nearly all have played a key role in the growth and development of our country, and many are celebrated in song and story. One could argue, however, that mile for mile none has had a greater economic, social, cultural, or political impact on our nation than the Hudson.

The Hudson River has its source in Lake Tear of the Clouds in the Adirondack Mountains. After descending southward very gradually over 315 miles, it empties into the Atlantic through one of the world's great natural harbors. From its "discovery" in 1524 by Giovanni da Verrazzano through Henry Hudson's visit in 1609 and the establishment of the colony of New Amsterdam in 1624, the potential of this harbor as a maritime center and of the river as a gateway to the American interior has been keenly appreciated.

Initially, river commerce focused on beaver pelts, but diversification came quickly by way of trade links to New England through the protected waters of Long Island Sound and to southern colonies along the coast. The opening of the Erie Canal in 1825, linking the Hudson to the Great Lakes by way of Albany and Buffalo, brought timber, grain, and other agricultural products to New York for export. Three years later the Delaware and Hudson Canal linked the Hudson to the coal fields of Pennsylvania and brought New York the fuel that powered its development as an industrial and manufacturing center. By the middle of the nineteenth century New York's place as America's largest and most dynamic city, its leading port, and its economic capital was secure. In 1860 more than half of all America's imports and exports passed through New York Harbor, and custom duties collected here covered virtually the entire cost of running the nation's government.

But the Hudson is not only a commercial corridor. From the seventeenth century onward, the river was recognized as a political and social boundary, marking the separation between English New England and the Dutch New Netherlands. The river was also an important link north through Lake George and Lake Champlain to Montreal and French Canada. Its strategic importance made the river hotly contested territory during both the French and Indian War and the American Revolution.

And it was in the Hudson Valley that American artists and writers first discovered and celebrated the beauty of our national landscape. Painters from Thomas Cole through Frederic Church vividly captured the river and scenic mountains that flank it. Writers, including Washington Irving, William Cullen Bryant, James Fenimore Cooper, and Walt Whitman, found inspiration in the history, landscape, and culture of the Hudson Valley. Contemporary authors and composers continue to celebrate the valley. Their works inspire not just Americans but visitors from around the world to seek out and enjoy the scenery along "America's Rhine."

The river, of course, was not always known as the Hudson. Formed during the Wisconsin glaciation between 26,000 and 13,000 years ago, the lower Hudson Valley is in fact a fjord carved by the retreating ice, part of a deep valley extending far out into the Atlantic beyond the current coastline. For thousands of years the river emptied into the ocean farther to the southwest, on the far side of the Palisades through the New Jersey meadows. Then about 6,000 years ago, thanks to an unknown geologic event, the river shifted to carve a new path through what is now the Narrows between Long Island and Staten Island to create today's harbor.

For over half of its length—as far north as Troy—the Hudson is a tidal estuary. Its flow changes direction, often quite dramatically, with the tides. The Lenape people who lived along the river's banks called it *Muhheakantuck*—the river that flows both ways. In addition to the river's southward freshwater flow, daily tidal action draws large quantities of salt water into the Hudson. This creates a remarkably rich and diverse natural ecosystem. When European settlers arrived, they found the river to be an abundant source of fish and particularly of oysters.

The Dutch called the Hudson the North River to distinguish it from the Delaware or South River and from the tidal straight that we today call the East River. The Hudson appellation occasionally appeared early on but came into general use only in the twentieth century. Today many maritime and municipal agencies, as well as a good number of maps, still refer to the lower section of the Hudson as the North River. (Beyond Albany, the Hudson name is almost universally applied.)

Today the Hudson remains a vital commercial and scenic waterway, but the nature of the traffic along and across the river has evolved dramatically over the years. The first big change came in 1807 when inventor and engineer Robert Fulton launched his steamboat the *Clermont*. Able to navigate the Hudson both with and against its powerful tides, steamboats transformed commercial and passenger transportation along the river. Beginning in the 1830s railway construction emerged as a faster and even more cost-effective method of moving passengers and goods, and by 1851 a line ran along the eastern bank of the Hudson all the way between Albany and New York. A second rail line on the river's western bank offered competing service, carrying vast quantities of raw materials, grain, and manufactured goods to and from New York Harbor. By 1867 Cornelius Vanderbilt had gained control of several formerly independent lines to form the New York Central system, a network of rails paralleling the Erie Canal and bracketing both sides of the Hudson.

In the mid-nineteenth century other railway companies established terminals along the western bank of the Hudson in Jersey City, Hoboken, and Weehawken to connect the port and the New York market with the American interior. These terminals were connected to Manhattan by a dense network of passenger and freight ferries across the river. By the early twentieth century the Hudson had also become the preferred docking location for transatlantic liners, and river traffic reached an extraordinary density.

In 1909 the Hudson and Manhattan Railway opened, providing passenger connections between Jersey City and Manhattan through tunnels under the river. Main-line service to Manhattan's new Pennsylvania Station followed a year later. Vehicular tunnels under the river arrived in due course: the Holland Tunnel in 1927 and the Lincoln Tunnel a decade later. The George Washington Bridge farther north opened in 1931. These connections made ferries increasingly redundant as passengers and freight flowed back and forth across the river through the bridges and tunnels. Steadily, Manhattan became less and less of an island.

In the 1950s the growth of transatlantic air service began to render passenger liners obsolete. Simultaneously the invention of containerized cargo ships drove freight from the Manhattan piers across the river to new, more modern terminals in New Jersey. River traffic on the Hudson declined dramatically and Manhattan, once a great port and manufacturing center, soon found itself to be neither. Piers were abandoned, warehouses sat empty, and once vital riverfront neighborhoods decayed. These seismic regional changes played a not-insignificant role in New York's 1975 municipal bankruptcy.

Happily, a waterfront renaissance—a reinvention—is underway. For the past 40 years New York has been step by step reclaiming and repurposing the banks of the Hudson. Abandoned piers have been removed or converted into parks, and new neighborhoods have been created on landfill. Old highways have been demolished and a former rail line converted into an elevated park. Thanks to the creation of the Hudson Greenway, it is now possible to walk or bike along the river almost all the way from the Battery to Spuyten Duyvil. The dynamic reinvention of the waterfront allows residents and visitors, for the first time since colonial days, to engage directly with the majestic river that is the key reason for our city's existence.

Figure I.2. The Hudson waterfront in 1932. *Source:* Geographic Guide. Public domain.

1

The Battery

New York's story begins at the southern tip of Manhattan Island. It is here that the city's two major waterways, the East River and the Hudson, converge to form one of the world's great harbors. This is where the Dutch established their initial settlement in 1626 and where they erected Fort Amsterdam, what became known as the Battery. Military fortifications dominated the southern tip of Manhattan Island well into the nineteenth century, but by 1840 a process of transformation was underway. In that year the city voted to create a 24-acre park here, primarily on landfill.

Manhattan island's original southern shoreline corresponded roughly to what is today State Street, and Fort Amsterdam sat at the edge of the harbor roughly on the site of what is now the Alexander Hamilton Custom House. The old fort was demolished shortly after the end of the Revolutionary War and was replaced in 1811 by a new one offshore on an artificial island. Beginning around 1855 the marshy areas at Manhattan's southern tip were slowly filled in with spoil from major street-widening and land-leveling projects to create much of what is today's park. By the 1870s visitors in large numbers came to enjoy fresh air and the view of the harbor by way of the elevated railway lines (Els) that converged on the park and upon the Staten Island Ferry Terminal nearby. While the El stations are a memory today, no less than six active subway lines have stations nearby.

Battery Park itself has been redesigned and extended multiple times over the years to provide additional space, to accommodate road construction, and to reflect evolving visions of the park's character and focus.

Figure 1.1. Map 1.

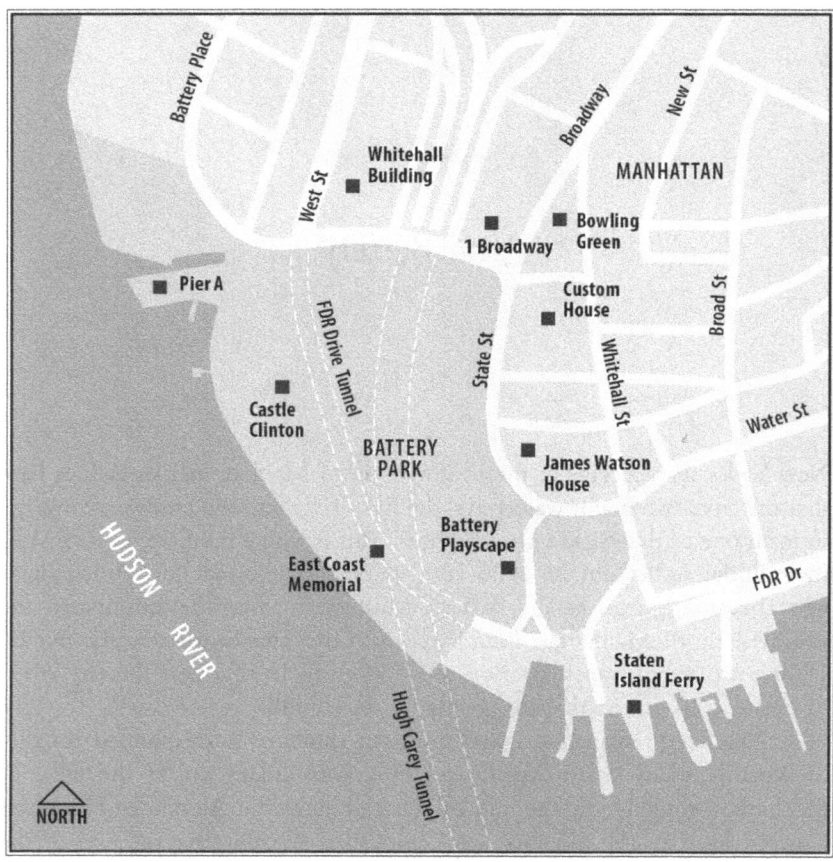

The most dramatic changes took place beginning in 1940 in conjunction with the construction of the Brooklyn-Battery Tunnel and the FDR Drive bypass beneath the park. (Happily, Robert Moses's plans for a suspension bridge linking the Battery and Brooklyn had been scotched.) In 1952 work was completed with the addition of an esplanade, relandscaping, and the creation of a waterfront terrace. By the 1980s, however, conditions in the park had deteriorated. A new master plan was approved by the city in 1986, and in 1994 the Battery Conservancy was created to coordinate ongoing public and private investment in the park. Major upgrades continue to this day, including repairs necessitated by damage sustained in 2012 during Hurricane Sandy.

Figure 1.2. Aerial view of the Battery, ca. 1928. *Source:* Alamy.

Today Battery Park offers matchless views of the harbor and a variety of attractions and memorials. It is a popular gathering spot for tourists, for Staten Island Ferry passengers, and for workers from nearby offices.

At the park's eastern end, the 1.5-acre **Battery Playscape** (2021; BKSK Architects and Starr Whitehouse Landscape Architects and Planners) seamlessly incorporates environmental and ecological education into a large, dynamic, and inviting children's playground. The park also includes Show Box, an inventive and flexible puppetry theater.

Nearby, the **Seaglass Carousel** (2015; WXY architecture + urban design; George Tsypin Opera Factory) simultaneously celebrates the park's history as the longtime home of the New York Aquarium and offers children a chance to ride inside one of 30 large fiberglass fish enveloped in an elaborate undersea light-and-sound environment. The carousel itself is housed in a futuristic architectural spiral inspired by the shape of a chambered nautilus.

To the west, the green expanse of the **Battery Oval** provides open spaces for picnics and recreation. The **Bosque Fountain** with its 35 programmed water jets stands near the **Battery Labyrinth**, a contemplative space commemorating the 9/11 World Trade Center attack. Nearby there is a woodland, a large perennial garden, and an urban farm.

The park has become a favored site for monuments and memorials, often focused on nautical and military subjects. At the center facing the harbor is a broad paved plaza with standing monoliths and a dramatically fierce bronze eagle. This is the **East Coast Memorial** (1963; Gehron & Seltzer, sculpture by Albino Manca) honoring the 4,600 American servicemembers who lost their lives in the Atlantic Ocean during World War II.

Not far off, at the foot of Pearl Street, the **Wireless Operators Memorial** (1915; Hewitt & Bottomley) was commissioned by public subscription to honor radio operators who died at sea while performing their duties. The first name on the list is that of Jack Phillips, radio operator on the *Titanic*. The **New York Korean War Veterans Memorial** (1991; Mac Adams), a 15-foot-tall granite stele at the west side of the park, includes a cutout silhouette of a walking soldier.

Figure 1.3. East Coast Memorial, Battery Park.

Nearby **The Immigrants** (1983; Luis Sanguino) is a dramatic and expressive group honoring the diverse range of arriving individuals who contributed so much to the character of the city. To the north, the **Netherland Monument** (1926; H. A. van den Eijnde) commemorates both the Dutch settlement of New Amsterdam and New York's particular origin story, the famous (or infamous) financial transaction between Governor Peter Minuit and the indigenous inhabitants of Manhattan.

There are also monuments honoring the Walloon settlers of New Amsterdam, Norwegian veterans, the Coast Guard, and individual immigrants who made significant contributions to their chosen home. There is an impressive statue of **Giovanni da Verrazzano** (1909; Ettore Ximenes) and one of John Ericsson, designer of the iron-clad USS *Monitor*. Plaques also honor engineer John Wolfe Ambrose, poet Emma Lazarus, Admiral George Dewey, and others. Quite a roster!

The **Castello Plan Monument** near the Staten Island Ferry terminal (2011; Simon Verity and Martha Finney) is a recreation in bronze of a celebrated historic map showing all 317 buildings extant in New York in the year 1660. Nearby there are bronze markers in the pavement indicating the evolving shape and location of the Battery's shoreline.

Figure 1.4. Castle Clinton (Castle Garden), 1901. *Source:* Library of Congress.

While all of these structures and memorials contribute to the park's distinctive character and personality, **Castle Clinton** dominates the site by its size and its history.

Few New York landmarks have so rich and colorful a story or have been put to such varied use. Castle Clinton began life as the West Battery during the War of 1812 and was renamed for New York Governor DeWitt Clinton in 1815. Lt. Col. Jonathan Williams and John Macomb Jr. designed the fort, which before landfill was added stood on an artificial island 300 feet offshore. Along with Castle Williams on nearby Governors Island and three other forts fronting the harbor, its job was to protect New York from a British invasion that never came. The city took over Castle Clinton 12 years after the war and converted it into Castle Garden, a concert venue and reception center for VIPs. It was here that Verdi's opera *Luisa Miller* had its American premiere. P. T. Barnum, however, orchestrated Castle Garden's greatest triumph—the much ballyhooed American debut on September 11, 1850, of vocalist Jenny Lind, the "Swedish Nightingale."

The fort became an immigrant processing station in 1855, and over the next 34 years more than eight million people entered the US here. (The site's importance to the history of immigration is reflected in the large number of monuments on this theme in Battery Park.) In 1890 the federal government took over immigrant processing from New York State and transferred operations to a new facility on Ellis Island two years later.

By 1896 Castle Clinton had been converted into the New York Aquarium, the first such facility in America. In 1921 the building received a major facelift designed by architects McKim, Mead & White. The aquarium was enormously popular and attracted huge crowds until it was closed and partially demolished by then–Parks Commissioner Robert Moses to make way for his planned bridge to Brooklyn. The aquarium eventually found a new home on Coney Island. The National Park Service took over in 1946, and today, after a long period of serious neglect, Castle Clinton has been restored to something like its original appearance. The completion of the Park Service's restoration in 1976 was celebrated with a special performance of Beethoven's Ninth Symphony by the New York Philharmonic, the same orchestra that had performed the American premiere of the work in Castle Garden in 1846. Today, after yet another renovation in 2010 by Beyer Blinder Belle & Thomas Phifer, Castle Clinton functions as the ticket office for tour boats to the Statue of Liberty and Ellis Island. (Try to ignore the ugly adjacent security screening facility for Statue of Liberty passengers.)

While Battery Park itself clearly has much to offer, the buildings that border it are also of real interest. At the far eastern end stands the bright, welcoming terminal of the **Staten Island Ferry** (2005; Schwartz Architects with Ron Evitts and TAMS), home to what is still New York's best sight-seeing bargain. A spectacular round trip ride across the harbor is free.

Just to the north at 7 State Street (once waterfront property) is the sole survivor of the row of elegant Federal period houses that graced this block at the turn of the nineteenth century. The **James Watson House/Rectory of the Shrine of St. Elizabeth Ann Seton** (1793–1806) is an elegant essay in brick and limestone.

An asymmetrical porch with thin, elongated Ionic columns, reputedly made from ship masts, carries the cornice around the street's curve. Note the fine crowning balustrade and the unusual oval windows on the west facade.

The house was originally built as the home of James Watson, first speaker of the New York State Assembly. In 1806 Watson sold his house to merchant Moses Rogers, who combined the Watson house with its neighbor to the west. The colonnade (attributed to John McComb Jr.) was added at this time to unite the two buildings. The Catholic Church acquired the structure in 1885

Figure 1.5. James Watson House.

as the site of a mission for young immigrant women. Today it is part of a shrine honoring the first native-born American to be canonized.

Emery Roth & Sons' far less elegant **17 State Street** (1987–1989) continues the westward curve of State Street, carrying the eye onward to one of New York's great Beaux Arts masterpieces, the **Alexander Hamilton Custom House** at 1 Bowling Green (1899–1907; Cass Gilbert).

Nearly every inch of the exterior is gloriously embellished. Daniel Chester French's *Four Continents* (1903–1907) stand guard out front, and inside there is a grand interior rotunda with paintings by Reginald Marsh. Today the building houses the National Museum of the American Indian and a federal bankruptcy court.

Across State Street, on the edge of Battery Park, is one of the only surviving original **control houses** providing entry to the New York subway. Erected in 1904 by architects Heins & LaFarge, the building is a charming concoction that blends modern utility with historic Dutch/Flemish detailing.

New York's first public park, **Bowling Green**, stands in front of the Custom House, still enclosed by its original fence from 1771. This is also the beginning point of Broadway, New York's most famous street. **Number 1 Broadway** (1882–1884; Edward H. Kendall; refaced 1919–1921 by Walter B. Chambers) is on the left.

Figure 1.6. Alexander Hamilton Custom House.

Figure 1.7. Number 1 Broadway.

This was long the home of the International Merchant Marine Company, parent of the United States Lines. The entry doors to the dedicated ticket offices for first- and cabin-class passengers can still be seen facing Battery Place.

To the west, past Aymar Embury II's austere and self-impressed **ventilation building** for the Brooklyn-Battery Tunnel (1950) is the **Whitehall Building** at 17 Battery Place (1902–1904; Henry J. Hardenbergh; expanded to the north in 1910 by Clinton & Russell).

Named for the mansion of Dutch Governor Peter Stuyvesant that once stood nearby, this 20-story office tower long dominated the southern tip of Manhattan. The architect of the original section, Henry Hardenbergh, went on to design the Plaza Hotel. Here he utilized a rich variety of materials, textures, and colors to create a structure that presents a bold, confident, and balanced face to the harbor. The Whitehall Building was an immediate success, and work was quickly begun on an even larger addition to the north. With its prospect on the harbor, this was long the home of

Figure 1.8. Whitehall Building. *Source:* Alamy.

the New York branch of the US Weather Bureau. It's worth noting that when the building was constructed, West Street along its western side was the edge of Manhattan Island.

The western, waterside boundary of Battery Park is marked by the affecting **American Merchant Mariners' Memorial** (1988–1991; Marisol Escobar) set on a stone breakwater in the harbor.

The artist based her design on a photograph taken by the crew of a German U-boat showing the survivors of a torpedoed American merchant ship clinging to the remains of their vessel. One member of the crew hangs off the edge of the breakwater and is submerged with each high tide.

On the Battery promenade just in front of the Merchant Mariners' Memorial, the metal railings are embellished with a series of inset panels. Entitled *River That Flows Two Ways*, these were installed by New York artist Wopo Holup in 2000. Running the entire length of the sea wall along the promenade, the 37 panels depict historic sites in lower Manhattan as well as river views and local wildlife. The title refers to the tidal character of the Hudson, where water flows not just down the river but in and out with the tides.

Figure 1.9. Merchant Mariners' Memorial.

Jutting out into the harbor just beyond the Mariners' Memorial is the picturesque **Pier A** (1884–1986; George Sears Greene Jr.; expanded 1900 and 1919; renovated 1999).

Built to house the city's Harbor Police and Docks Department, this was also the longtime headquarters of the Marine Division of the New York City Fire Department (FDNY). In more recent years the building has been adapted into a food court and restaurant. It is currently again under restoration. Designed by the Docks Department's chief engineer, the building, unlike most of its now vanished contemporaries, sits on an elaborate foundation of concrete and granite piers. The clock in the tower overlooking the Hudson is a memorial to the fallen in World War I and is one of only a few remaining waterfront clocks that continue to strike the hours in nautical time.

Figure 1.10. Pier A.

The Hudson Docks: 1624 to Today

At Pier A the leafy openness of Battery Park gives way to the Hudson waterfront, long the center of maritime activity in New York. Most of the world's great cities are built on rivers: Think of London, Paris, Amsterdam, Venice, St. Petersburg, or Shanghai. In each instance, the city's grandest public buildings are oriented to the water, creating a ceremonial entry to the metropolis. New York is different. As a comparatively new island city that literally owed its existence to maritime trade, waterfront commerce took center stage. From the start Manhattan's riverbanks were a place of business: a place for docks, warehouses, chandleries, shipyards, foundries, railway yards, taverns, boarding houses, and brothels. Such establishments, although not decorative, were the lifeblood of the city and received shoreline priority. Public buildings and private residences were located at the center of the island, as far from the noise and dirt of the waterfront as possible.

New York's waterfront is distinctive in other ways as well. Its harbor remains relatively ice-free for the entire winter, it is not plagued by ocean fog, and it is blessed with naturally occurring ship channels. Also, unlike such major ports as London, Liverpool, and Amsterdam where harbor water levels rise and fall dramatically with the tides, water depth in New York Harbor remains comparatively constant. Where other ports require closed docks to ensure that ships remain afloat, New York's more moderate tides permit continuously accessible open wharfs. In addition, while closed-basin docks are major engineering projects that typically depend on government support for their construction; open wharfs are comparatively simple to build. New York capitalized on this fact. Until the mid-nineteenth century, the city allowed its shoreline to be privately developed.

Under New York's 1731 City Charter (known as the Montgomerie Charter after the British governor who issued it), the city was granted ownership of all underwater land extending out 400 feet from the shore at the river's low tide line. New York early on sold "water lots" between the tide line and this 400-foot mark to private individuals. Purchasers could build wharfs and add fill for pierheads and warehouses. They were expected to properly maintain these facilities in return for the right to collect docking fees. In practice, however, the city retained little practical control over the condition of its waterfront, and dock conditions quickly deteriorated. Sanitation was also an issue. The city's sewage was dumped directly into the river, where it accumulated in the Hudson docks to depths of five feet per year. In fact, a misguided early ordinance passed in the 1730s actually required citizens to throw trash and sewage into the rivers to prevent them from fouling the streets!

Although the process of adding landfill, bulkheads, and docks along the Hudson began as early as 1811, it was not until mid-century that the center of gravity of New York's maritime world relocated there from its original home on the East River, where dock space and maneuvering room in the river were more limited. Construction along the Hudson exploded, spurred by New York's increasingly dominant position as America's leading port. (In 1835, out of 240 ships sailing from Liverpool to the US, 168 docked in New York.) By the time of the Civil War, the banks of the Hudson were a hodgepodge of rickety wooden piers of differing lengths and designs. Selective filling and haphazard, unplanned development meant that there was no consistent bulkhead or quay line.

Faced with deteriorating dock conditions, and rightly fearful that commerce would relocate to better managed facilities elsewhere, the city took action. In 1870 it established a Department of Docks and began to slowly buy back control of its waterfront and to establish new and consistent standards for the length and depth of berths. In 1871 Civil War general and engineer George McClellan was recruited to manage the creation of a uniform granite-faced bulkhead from the Battery all the way north to 61st Street along the Hudson shore. The bulkhead was designed to rise six feet above the high-water line and extend 20 feet below. The project also included landfill to create a new avenue to service the waterfront. The scope of the project was enormous, and progress was slow. It took over 60 years to complete.

As the nineteenth century progressed, passenger and freight vessels grew ever larger. The creation of piers long enough to accommodate them, however, was stymied by the Montgomerie Charter, which gave the city control offshore only to the 400-foot mark. Beyond that point the Army Corps of Engineers was in charge. In the name of keeping the channel open for naval defense, the Corps refused to allow piers to be lengthened farther into the river. The city's only solution was to move eastward and to "rewater" previously filled water lots.

As a result of these interventions, the shape of Manhattan Island has for over 300 years been in a constant state of flux. The shoreline looks very

Figure 1.11. Detail of the Viele map of Manhattan. *Source:* Library of Congress, Geography and Map Division. Public domain.

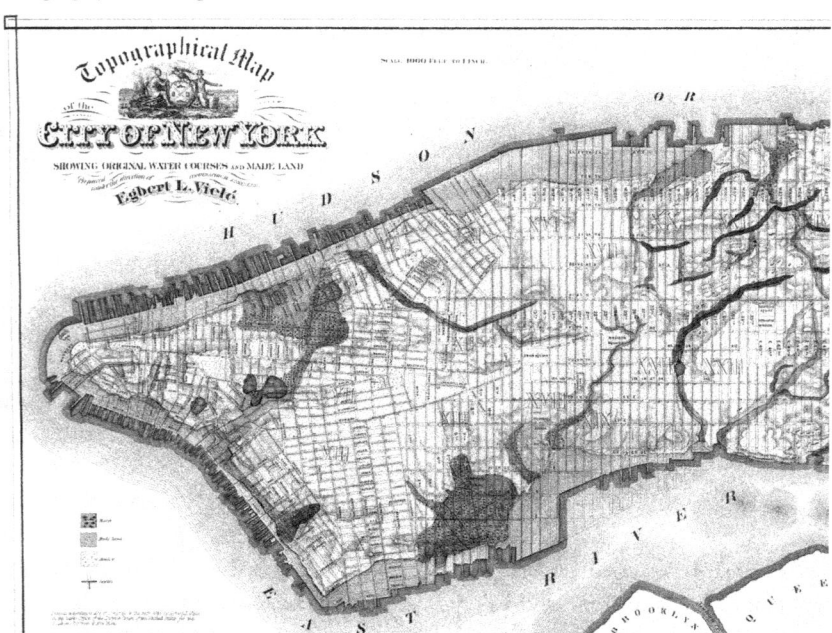

different today than it did 1624 when the Dutch arrived. In 1660 when the Castello Plan of New Amsterdam was drawn, Manhattan's Hudson shoreline was located roughly 800 feet to the east of its current location, along what is now Greenwich Street. The speed of change can be clearly seen on Egbert Viele's celebrated topographical map of New York from 1865, which clearly shows the original shoreline, filled land, and piers.

By the turn of the twentieth century the Hudson waterfront was teeming, a continuous five-mile row of docks serving cargo and passenger ships, as well as a flotilla of ferries shuttling railway cars and human passengers back and forth across the river. The docks were supported by a dense network of warehouses, rail lines, and other services filling the city blocks immediately inland. The congestion was formidable as trucks, wagons, trains, and pedestrians contended. Fatalities were frequent.

In front of the docks along the stretch of West Street and 12th Avenue from the Battery to 72nd Street there were over 100 railway grade crossings. The street's nickname, "Death Avenue," was richly deserved. To reduce congestion, the city proposed a twofold solution: an elevated freight railway and a parallel elevated highway. Construction of the High Line railway (about which more will be said later) was completed in 1934 with trains running on a trestle from the St. John's Terminal at Washington and Houston Streets to huge rail yards at 35th Street.

Figure 1.12. West Street, 1901. *Source:* Library of Congress, Prints and Photographs Division, Detroit Publishing Company Collection. Public domain.

To address the issue of vehicular traffic congestion, work on what would be dubbed the Miller Highway (after its champion, Manhattan Borough President Julius Miller) began in 1929 and continued in sections until 1951.

One of the first elevated highways built in the United States, the limited-access Miller Highway ran parallel to the river following West Street, 11th Avenue, and 12th Avenue from Battery Place north to 72nd Street. The highway, with its narrow lanes and awkward left-hand exits, was problematic from the start and deferred maintenance quickly took its toll. In December of 1973 a section of the roadway near Gansevoort Street collapsed. A year later the entire highway south of 46th Street was closed to traffic, and demolition began. The northern stretch just south of 59th Street was demolished in 1989. The Miller Highway's active life was barely 25 years.

By 1930 New York City had become the world's busiest port. During daylight hours a ship arrived or departed every 10 minutes. Shipping lines served 159 foreign routes as well as many intercoastal destinations. The Works Progress Administration (WPA) guide to New York City eloquently described the Hudson waterfront in those years:

Figure 1.13. Miller Highway, 1931. *Source:* Courtesy Municipal Archives, City of New York. Used with permission.

Although the western rim of Manhattan is but a small section of New York's far-flung port, along it is concentrated the largest aggregate of marine enterprises in the world. Glaciers of freight and cargo move across this strip of . . . waterfront. It is the domain of the superliner, but it is shared by the freighter, the river boat, the ferry, and the soot-faced tug. . . . Ships and shipping are not visible along much of West Street. South of Twenty-Third Street, the river is walled by an almost unbroken line of bulkhead sheds and dock structures. . . . Opposite the piers, along the entire length of the highway, nearly every block houses its quota of cheap lunchrooms, tawdry saloons and waterfront haberdasheries catering to the thousands of polyglot seamen who haunt the front. Men "on the beach" (out of employment) usually make their headquarters in barrooms, which are frequented mainly by employees of lines leasing piers in their vicinity. . . . This is the most lucrative water-front property in the world. (Federal Writers Project, *New York City Guide*, 1939)

Figure 1.14. West Street and Hudson Piers, 1916. *Source:* New York Public Library. Public domain.

Twenty years later, the situation was very different. The debut of the container ship in 1956 and the resulting decline of traditional break-bulk cargo quickly rendered Manhattan's piers obsolete. In short order, operations were relocated across the river to Port Newark and Port Elizabeth, where containers could be easily transferred directly to trains or trucks for onward shipping. At the same time, steadily growing airline service signaled the ultimate decline of transatlantic passenger liners while rail and vehicular tunnels under the river dramatically reduced the need for passenger and car ferries. The result was a dramatic decrease in river traffic.

By the 1970s, the Hudson waterfront, once vital, was reduced to a string of dilapidated and rotting piers, deserted rail lines, deteriorating highways, and empty warehouses. What had been a thriving and vital commercial district was largely deserted, and the inhabitants of Manhattan found themselves cut off by a ring of blight from the river that was once their city's raison d'être. The story of what has happened since begins with the creation of Battery Park City.

2

Battery Park City

As you round the corner from Pier A and head north along the Hudson shoreline, nearly all the land for the next mile is man-made, a self-contained 92-acre neighborhood. The story of its creation begins with a mid-twentieth-century effort to revitalize lower Manhattan. Downtown has always been the nerve center of New York's business world, but by the 1950s this identity was threatened by the simultaneous development of new office buildings in midtown and by the decline of traditional commerce along the Hudson River docks. City officials and downtown landlords were both concerned.

In 1960 David Rockefeller took action, commissioning a huge and glossy new headquarters between Pine and Liberty Streets for **Chase Manhattan Bank**, of which he was the chairman. His investment was a powerful expression of confidence in the future of lower Manhattan. Other businesses, which might have considered relocating uptown, took note. Rockefeller and his high-powered colleagues on the Downtown–Lower Manhattan Association also took the lead in pressing for zoning changes that would encourage the construction of housing in lower Manhattan, a crucial step in making the area, long deserted after five o'clock, a true 24-hour "walk to work" neighborhood.

Six years later, pressed by both David Rockefeller and his brother, New York Governor Nelson Rockefeller, the Port Authority of New York and New Jersey broke ground for the twin towers of the **World Trade Center**. The huge complex shifted the center of gravity of lower Manhattan westward toward the Hudson. Upon its completion in 1975 an average of 50,000 people reported for work there every day.

Figure 2.1. Map 2.

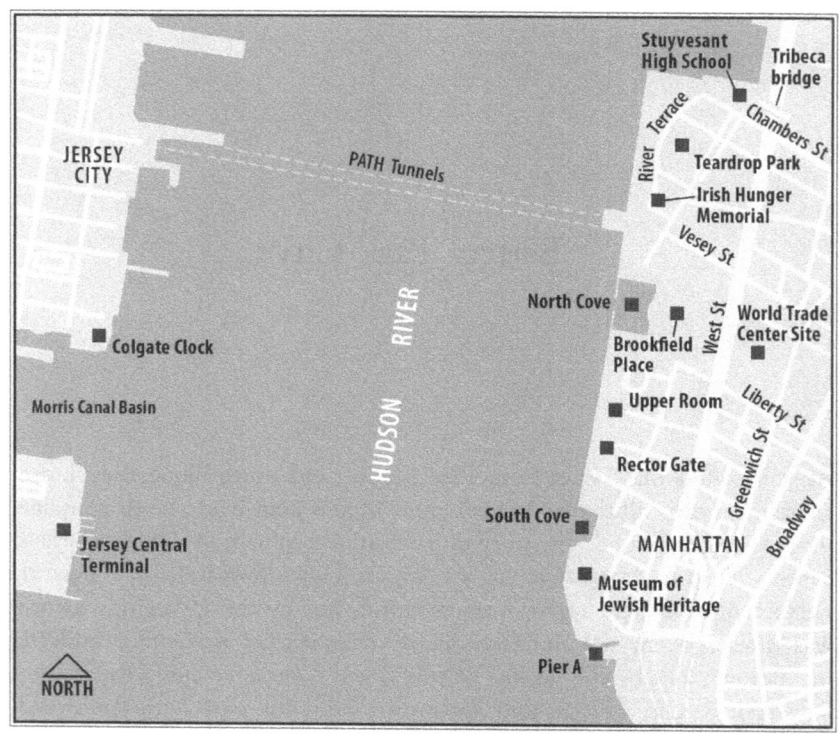

Figure 2.2. World Trade Center, ca. 1990. *Source:* Alamy.

Excavations for the two 110-story towers, the surrounding buildings, and for a large central plaza generated huge amounts of rubble. The Port Authority used that material to create new land, filling in water lots in the Hudson long occupied by now disused piers. (Additional fill came from dredging the Ambrose Channel in Lower New York Bay and from the construction of the city's Water Tunnel 3.) The newly created land covered 92 acres, stretching along the river from Pier A to Chambers Street. The stage was set for the creation of **Battery Park City**.

Actual development, however, took some time. Meanwhile, the vast, unimproved site became a popular place for New Yorkers to sunbathe, play, and relax. There were concerts and temporary art installations, and at one point environmental artist Agnes Dene planted a field of summer wheat on two acres of the site.

In 1967 the New York State legislature, again with key support from the Rockefellers, created the Battery Park City Authority and charged it with the development of the filled land. The Authority initially envisioned a futuristic community that mixed commercial, residential, and supporting retail development in megastructures and superblocks with elevated walkways separating cars and pedestrians.

Figure 2.3. Battery Park City site, ca. 1980. *Source:* Battery Park City Authority.

Happily, that vision for a radically new kind of urban environment went nowhere. Over the following decade, plans were continually revised, pushed back and forth by political, real estate, and financial wrangling. Finally, in 1979 with the Authority facing bankruptcy, a new design firm was engaged to create a simpler, more workable development plan. This scheme, prepared by Alexander Cooper and Stanton Eckstut, reversed the thinking of previous designs. Instead of rejecting the character of the existing city, their plan embraced it.

The Cooper-Eckstut design replaced megastructures with informal groupings of smaller buildings interspersed with parks and public spaces. Although Battery Park City was separated from existing neighborhoods by broad and busy West Street, the designers emulated the irregular layout of downtown by specifying informal, sometimes curving streets and by dotting their plan with small parks. No two blocks were alike. The emphasis was on variety, on the creation of unique and independent mini-neighborhoods linked by a shared waterfront esplanade. The plan provided for 26 separate parcels of land. Each was to be independently developed in accordance with a set of rigid design guidelines covering building size, placement, and materials. The overall Cooper-Eckstut site plan anchored Battery Park City just to the west the World Trade Center with a major complex of office towers and a high-end shopping mall. The areas to the north and south were set aside for residential development, and a full one-third of the acreage was allocated to parks and open space.

Development proceeded in stages beginning in 1981 with the commercial core. Shortly after, the Authority released the area around Rector Place for residential development. Battery Place to the south was next, with construction beginning in 1985. Stuyvesant High School at the extreme north end of the complex went up in 1992, and two years later the surrounding North Residential Area was opened for development with slightly revised guidelines prepared by Ralph Lerner. The last section to be completed was that to the south, abutting Battery Park itself. By 2020 Battery Park City included more than 50 separate buildings. It is home to 14,000 residents, 10 million square feet of office space, three schools, 36 acres of parks, and a 1.2-mile riverfront esplanade. While some critics have labeled the carefully planned development "suburban" in feel, its popularity as a desirable place to both live and work is undeniable.

Just to the north of Pier A, a narrow inlet separates the Battery from **Robert F. Wagner, Jr. Park**. Originally designed in 1996 (OLIN, with

Figure 2.4. Battery Park City in 2022. *Source:* Battery Park City Authority.

Lynden Miller and Machado & Silvestri) as a gateway to Battery Park City, the 3.5-acre park is currently in the midst of a major rebuilding to protect it from rising sea levels. The updated park will remain focused on a central pavilion housing a restaurant, restrooms, and a rooftop terrace offering panoramic views of the harbor—including a carefully framed vista of the Statue of Liberty. On the river side the building will overlook a terraced lawn with low seating walls surveying the water. There will be lushly planted gardens to either side of the central features, punctuated by commissioned sculptures including Jim Dine's *Ape and Cat at the Dance*, 1996; Louise Bourgeoise's *Eyes*, 1998; and Tony Cragg's *Resonating Bodies*, 1996 (these are at present temporarily relocated farther north).

While construction is underway, Pier A is a great location from which to survey the harbor. Off to the left is **Governor's Island**. The 172-acre island is now a park offering a range of public programs and a great view back to the Manhattan skyline. In earlier years its history was military. First fortified in 1741, the island remained an important strongpoint for harbor defense well into the nineteenth century. Long the headquarters of the US First Army, Governor's Island was transferred to the Coast Guard in 1965. The Guard moved out in 1995, and in 2003 the title to the land was transferred to a joint city-state agency for public use.

Beyond Governor's Island, off in the distance one can make out the towers of **Verrazzano Narrows Bridge** (1964; Othmar Ammann) linking Brooklyn to Staten Island and marking the spot were New York's upper and lower bays meet. Hilly Staten Island is bordered on the north by Kill van Kull, through which cargo vessels pass on their way to the container terminals in Newark Bay. Additional shipping terminals are visible in Bayonne behind the **Statue of Liberty**. To the right of Miss Liberty is **Ellis Island**, from 1892 to 1954 America's primary processing center for immigrants. During those years over 12 million immigrants arrived here. Long abandoned, today the key buildings (1900; Boring & Tilton) have been restored as a museum of immigration, a component of the Statue of Liberty National Monument.

At the northern end of Wagner Park, **The Museum of Jewish Heritage** (1993–1997, expanded 2003; Kevin Roche, John Dinkeloo & Associates) dominates the waterfront. The museum's story begins in 1947 with a plan to build a city memorial to the victims of the Holocaust. Many proposals were considered and abandoned. Then in 1985 Governor Mario Cuomo offered this site at the southern end of Battery Park City. Construction on the initial building, a massive, somber granite hexagon with a stepped six-tiered roof, began in 1994, and the museum opened three years later. In 2000 construction began on a major addition by the same architects. The new building, named in honor of New York Attorney General Robert Morganthau (who was also the museum's chairman), curves protectively around the earlier structure, to which it is linked. Lighter, sleeker, and more angular than the original memorial, the new building houses a theater, café, galleries, offices, and classrooms. There is a raised terrace between the two buildings where sculptor Andy Goldsworthy has created a remarkable landscape of intertwined boulders and oak trees. Inside, the permanent exhibition on the Holocaust is as comprehensive as it is moving.

Just across Battery Place, the curving facade of **2 West Street** (2001; Gary Edward Handel + Associates and the Polshek Partnership) nicely complements that of the museum. The lower wing of the building originally housed a Ritz-Carlton hotel. Today the tower to the east houses

Figure 2.5. Museum of Jewish Heritage.

condominium residences. From the harbor's edge the building provides an effective backdrop to Wagner Park, while its massing and materials pay homage to the older Whitehall Building nearby. 2 West Street is also the home of the fascinating **Skyscraper Museum** (2004; Skidmore Owings & Merrill). The entry is located at street level at 39 Battery Place, facing the Museum of Jewish Heritage. Exhibitions inside document the history of New York City's most celebrated building type. To the north, Handel's **30 Little West Street** (2007) and Cesar Pelli's more elegant **70 Little West Street** (2008) establish a rear wall for this section of Battery Park City along West Street.

Just to the north of the museum and back toward the river is the **Mother Cabrini Memorial** (2020; Jill and Giancarlo Biagi) facing out across the harbor toward Ellis Island. Maria Francesca Cabrini, known as Mother Frances Xavier Cabrini, was the founder of the Missionary Sisters of the Sacred Heart. She emigrated from Italy to the United States in 1889 and devoted her life to assisting immigrants, of whom she is the patron saint. The cast bronze reliefs around the base of the memorial depict significant events in her life. A woman of formidable energy and organizational ability, Cabrini founded 67 orphanages, schools, and hospitals in New York and around the world. She was the first naturalized American to be canonized and is buried at a shrine in upper Manhattan.

The Cabrini Memorial marks the beginning of the **South Cove**, one of two such basins in Battery Park City.

South Cove (1988) is primarily the work of artist Mary Miss, acting in collaboration with Stanton Eckstut and landscape designer Susan Child. One enters the cove through an area of dense plantings to emerge on a curving pergola-sheltered wooden pier that extends out over the water. To the right a bowed wooden bridge heads eastward toward a black steel observation platform designed to recall the crown of the Statue of Liberty.

Figure 2.6. South Cove, Battery Park City.

On one side of the bridge Miss has removed the landfill to reveal the river and the concrete foundations of former piers. On the other side is a small island garden of native plants. The path continues around the cove flanked by wooden railings and strewn boulders seemingly placed at random. Offshore, wooden pilings of diminishing height in the water assist the visual transition from land to river and are another reminder of the busy maritime culture once centered here. With its evocation of times past, its dense plantings, and its studied rusticity, the cove feels somehow set apart, private, almost romantic—a place to pause and catch one's breath.

50 and **70 Battery Place** stand to the east of the cove, a pair of understated nine-story apartment buildings by Hardy Holzman Pfeiffer (1999). Just ahead is a small square marking the downtown end of South End Avenue, one of Battery Park City's main thoroughfares. On the right at 2 South End Avenue is the **Cove Club Apartments** (1991; Polshek & Partners) with their bay windows carefully angled to maximize the view. To the left at 21 South End Avenue is the larger **Regatta Apartments** (1989; Gruzen Samton Steinglass) organized around an open central courtyard. If none of these buildings are of more than routine architectural interest, this was, to a degree, by design. From the start, the emphasis at Battery Park City was on the park. As the guidelines stated, "The public spaces of the streets and parks are the emphasis of the design work and the focus of the new development. The buildings are the background." Guidelines regulated the bulk and height of buildings on each lot to ensure good light and to maximize views over the harbor. All buildings were required to begin with a two-story stone base. Warm or neutral colored brick was specified for the areas above. Metal, glass, and concrete were discouraged. Buildings were intended to be modest, to fit in, to be good neighbors.

The entire Battery Park City complex is linked together by the 1.2-mile-long **Battery Park City Esplanade**.

Cooper and Eckstut drew heavily on successful New York prototypes for their designs, including the Brooklyn Heights Promenade. The hexagonal asphalt pavers and lampposts are the same as those used around Central Park, and the curving black steel railing set on a granite base along the water is reassuringly solid yet graceful.

One of the esplanade's most distinctive and successful features is its two-level design. On the landward side the shaded and lushly planted walkway is slightly elevated. Down two steps toward the water is a second promenade. Here the emphasis is on openness, sunshine, and views of the

Figure 2.7. Battery Park City Esplanade.

harbor. The benches here are lighter and more open than those above. Signage directs bicyclists and skaters to the lower walkway, and walkers to the upper.

Moving northward, the east–west streets of Battery Park City terminate at the esplanade. From the start, planners saw these intersections as mini-parks and as sites for commissioned artworks. At the foot of West Thames Street **Sitting/Stance** (1988; Richard Artschwager) is a playfully surreal grouping of overscaled furniture in redwood and granite. Nearby a New York streetlamp has been removed from its usual tall post to become the centerpiece of a circular table.

The urban embellishments are somewhat grander one block north at Rector Place. Here the focus is R. M. Fischer's **Rector Gate** (1988), a 45-foot tall sci-fi/Erector-set construction with a quirky charm. Critic Nancy Princenthal accurately described it as "equal parts Samurai warrior and Buck Rogers."

To the east the two lanes of Rector Place are separated by **Rector Park**, a quiet, old-fashioned pair of one-acre spaces designed in 1985 by Richard Webel with Vollmer Associates.

The western end of Rector Place is framed by two tall apartment houses: **Liberty Terrace** (1987; Ulrich Franzen/The Vilkas Group) to the south at 380 Rector Place, and **Liberty House** (1986; James Stewart

Figure 2.8. Rector Gate, Battery Park City.

Polshek & Partners) at 377 Rector Place to the north. Both terminate in broad angled facades that frame the start of the street. Each architect has attempted to conform to Battery Park City guidelines while giving their structure a distinct personality. Franzen does so quietly, Polshek uses bolder polychromy.

At the next corner, the intersection of the esplanade and Albany Street, we are transported to the banks of the Nile by way of Ned Smythe's **Upper Room** (1987).

A broken colonnade of abstracted and pebble-encrusted Egyptian columns surrounds an outdoor room. At the center a baldachin shelters a decorated mosaic palm tree. Nearby is a long table inlaid with chess boards,

Figure 2.9. Upper Room, Battery Park City.

awaiting players. The temple is a whimsical blend of the mysterious and quotidian, the ceremonial and domestic.

A few steps to the east at **320–340 Albany Street** architects Davis, Brody & Associates (1986) have created a remarkably successful row of townhouses that riffs on the traditional New York brownstone—complete with front stoops, bay windows, and even the suggestion of a cornice.

Moving north, the next group of buildings, **Gateway Plaza** (1982–1983; Jack Brown and Irving E. Gershon) is a discordant note. This was the first complex to be developed in Battery Park City, and the project gained approval before the Cooper-Eckstut design guidelines were formally adopted. The pale, grim, self-contained superblock with its interconnected towers resembles a half-hearted urban renewal project.

Just to the north of Gateway Plaza the esplanade opens into the **North Cove**, a richly complex space that is the commercial and retail center of Battery Park City.

The four massive towers of what was originally dubbed the **World Financial Center** (1981–1988; Cesar Pelli & Associates) and is today known as **Brookfield Place** are loosely grouped around the cove and its yacht basin. Access from the World Trade Center site is provided by pedestrian bridges and tunnels across West Street. These terminate in two octagonal

Figure 2.10. North Cove, Battery Park City.

"gatehouses" that lead to an elevated concourse containing high-end retail shops and connect the office towers to a barrel-vaulted Winter Garden.

Before the tragic attack of September 11, 2001, the buildings of the World Financial Center sat directly to the west of the World Trade Center, the twin towers of which dominated the lower Manhattan skyline. Pelli was faced with the challenge of the overwhelming scale and presence of these two isolated behemoths. His solution was to draw inspiration from the classic skyscraper forms of the past. At ground level his buildings are solid, clad in granite. As they rise the towers open visually. Windows become larger, the stone is a lighter color, and carefully stepped setbacks create an attractive upward pull that does much to lighten the appearance of buildings that can appear squat and massive. Each building's profile is subtly different, and each tower has been given an individual copper crown—a shallow dome, a pyramid, a mastaba. The buildings range in height from 34 to 51 stories, and Pelli was careful to arrange them to lead the eye upward to the Trade

Center towers. In doing so he took an important step toward reestablishing the traditional profile of the lower Manhattan skyline, stepping up gracefully from the water to taller buildings inland. Today the twin towers are gone, but the Pelli complex still provides the same framing for the new Freedom Tower.

The architect's **Winter Garden**, rebuilt in 2002 after being damaged in the Trade Center attack, has been rightly likened to both the Crystal Palace and the interior of Grand Central Terminal. It provides an elegant transition from the elevated concourse linking the commercial towers to the cove and esplanade. Interior corridors lined with shops and food services branch out in all directions. At the center under the soaring 120-foot-tall arch of glass and steel, a flight of pink marble steps cascades down toward the river through a grove of palm trees. The highly polished staircase is often called into service for staged photographs and as a platform for performance events. The theatricality of the space adds welcome drama to what is essentially a suburban shopping mall.

Figure 2.11. Winter Garden, Brookfield Place.

Outside, the **North Cove** itself is a busy and complex place. At its center is a large yacht harbor, protected by a breakwater. Berths are available for rental, and there are excursion boats of various types for hire. At the southeast corner of the boat basin is the eloquent, understated **New York City Police Memorial** (1997; Stuart Crawford). A sunken pool fed by a small waterfall is flanked by a polished granite wall bearing the names of New York police officers who have lost their lives in the line of duty. A carefully placed bench completes the handsomely composed and satisfying composition. Nearby, tucked up against the north wall of Gateway Plaza is something quite different, a fragment of the **Berlin Wall**—dismantled in 1989 and installed here in 2004 as a gift from the German Consulate.

The plazas surrounding the North Cove were designed by artists Scott Burton and Siah Armajani and are separated into three zones, each with its own distinct personality. At the south, nestled into the Financial Center where it intersects with Liberty Street, is a secluded tree-ringed grass oval area known as **Pumphouse Park**, originally the site of huge conduits and pumps that served the Trade Center complex. Flowering cherry trees flank a gravel walkway, punctuated with teak benches designed by Burton. Immediately to the north, Pumphouse Park merges into an enclosed garden with lushly planted seasonal beds separated by wandering paths.

This garden gives way to a broad, paved, multilevel central area opening onto the yacht harbor. Café tables spill out onto a shaded, raised veranda bordered by a 150-foot-long fountain. At either end, steps and ramps lead down to a lower plaza, curving out into the basin and anchored by a standing beacon designed by Armajani. Here, close to the harbor, there are massive polished pink granite benches designed by Burton. Looking west from these benches, the view of the water is partially interrupted by a handsome bronze and green painted fence bearing poems by Walt Whitman and Frank O'Hara spelled out in bronze letters.

Inland, the carefully composed ring of skyscrapers provides a dramatic backdrop. The North Cove is a remarkably lively urban space, nearly always filled with a dynamic mix of tourists, shoppers, and office workers taking a break. Burton and Armajani have provided a full range of spaces, each with its own personality, to suit a full range of visitor moods. (Note: As with Wagner Park to the south, the North Cove is scheduled for a major redesign to improve storm resiliency. As of early 2024 specific plans were still under development.)

The uptown end of the North Cove is anchored by yet another distinct urban landscape. **The Belvedere** (1995; Mitchell/Giurgola with Child Associates) was designed to bridge the gap between the hard stonescape of the North Cove and the broad lawns of Rockefeller Park to the north and to serve as a gateway to a new Hudson River ferry terminal. From a tree-shaded terrace at the foot of North End Avenue, one descends by broad steps to the main level of the esplanade. Straight ahead facing the Hudson are a handsome pair of sculptures, the ***Pylons*** (1995; Martin Puryear).

One of the stainless steel towers is solid, formed of stacked inverted pyramids that diminish in size as they rise. The other is an open lattice of tapered cylinders that spirals upward. The sculptures were originally designed to frame the entrance to the ferry landing stage. With the construction of a permanent ferry landing slightly to the north, Puryear's dignified works now stand on their own.

Just to the north of the Belvedere is **300 Vesey Street** (1997; SOM). Built as a new headquarters for the venerable New York Mercantile Exchange,

Figure 2.12. Martin Puryear, *Pylons*.

the building has now been incorporated into Brookfield Place. In their design Skidmore, Owings & Merrill were careful to echo the materials, fenestration, and massing of the Pelli complex while simultaneously providing a broad sweeping curved wall of windows facing the river to the west. The understated building works to create a smooth transition from the riverbank to the earlier Brookfield Place complex to the east.

The **Brookfield Place/Battery Park City Ferry Terminal** (2009; FTL Happold) has a long history. Ferries across the Hudson date back at least to 1661. Before the construction of rail and tunnel links across the river, they were essential to New York commerce, and multiple lines provided connections to multiple destinations. The last passenger ferries from lower Manhattan to railway terminals in Jersey City and Hoboken ceased to operate in the late 1960s. Slips were demolished and boats retired. The ferries were missed, but it took until 1986 and the completion of the World Financial Center for service to be restored to Vesey Street. The current terminal was completed in 2009. The new dock was constructed in Texas and floated into place. With its transparent steel and glass superstructure and sail-like tensile roof it is both elegant and well suited to its purpose. Today one can catch boats from here to Jersey City, Hoboken, Weehawken, Edgewater, and Midtown Manhattan.

Figure 2.13. Brookfield Place Ferry Terminal.

The ferry terminal is an excellent place to pause and look out across the river to the far bank. Just to the north of Ellis Island is the handsome spire and red brick facade of the former **Central Railway of New Jersey Terminal** in Jersey City (1899; Peabody & Stearns).

During its heyday in the early twentieth century, the station, located at the mouth of the Morris Canal linking the Delaware and Hudson Rivers, lay at the center of the vast Communipaw Rail Yard. The terminal was also an important passenger depot, serving not just the Jersey Central but the Reading and Baltimore & Ohio (B&O) Railways as well. Over half of the immigrants processed on Ellis Island moved by special ferry from the island to this terminal to begin the next phase of their journey. Today the old terminal is a part of New Jersey's Liberty State Park and offers ferry service to the Statue of Liberty.

Just to the north of the Morris Canal basin in the Paulus Hook section of Jersey City is the landmark **Colgate Clock**. At the time of its original installation the clock was reputedly the largest in the world. From 1924 until 1985 the clock stood atop a huge Colgate-Palmolive soap factory about 400 yards to the north. Its shape was chosen to remind viewers of the Colgate firm's signature product: Octagon Detergent. When the Colgate plant closed, its site was redeveloped, and the monumental clock was relocated to its present position.

The flat land along the western side of the Hudson was long the home of rail yards, factories, warehouses, and docks. As economic needs changed these were abandoned, and the area has been dramatically transformed into

Figure 2.14. Jersey Central Railway Terminal.

a dense concentration of office and apartment buildings, hotels, and urban amenities. Due to the number of financial firms that have located here, the area has been dubbed Wall Street West. The redeveloped riverfront communities are linked by the Hudson–Bergen Light Rail line running from Bayonne all the way to Weehawken. There is also an 18.5-mile riverfront walkway. In addition to ferries, Jersey City is connected to downtown Manhattan, Newark, and Hoboken by PATH (Port Authority Trans-Hudson) trains. These were the first rail tunnels to pass beneath the Hudson. Originally built as the Hudson & Manhattan Railroad in 1909, the system was designed to link the Erie, Lackawanna, and Pennsylvania rail terminals in New Jersey with destinations in Manhattan. The line was taken over by the Port Authority in 1962 when the railroad's original Manhattan terminus was demolished to make way for the World Trade Center. The line's downtown branch runs directly under the Brookfield Place ferry terminal to terminate at Santiago Calatrava's white-ribbed Oculus, adjacent to the World Trade Center site.

The availability of cross-Hudson rail and ferry transportation has been a key factor in Jersey City's renaissance. Immediately to the north of the Colgate Clock is the 42-story **Goldman Sachs Tower** at 30 Hudson Street (2004; Cesar Pelli). For many years it was the tallest building in New Jersey and was intended to be the centerpiece of a large Goldman Sachs campus in Jersey City. Manhattan-based executives were, however, reluctant to relocate, so the firm built a second tower in New York just to the north of Brookfield Place instead. Goldman Sachs long sponsored a special ferry to shuttle employees back and forth across the river.

Perhaps the second most eye-catching building on the packed waterfront is the **Jersey City Urby Apartments** at 200 Greene Street (2016; HLW architects). It is 68 stories tall with a distinctive silhouette of shifting, cantilevered blocks of floors.

Back on the Manhattan side, just to the north of the Ferry Terminal at the point where Vesey Street intersects with the esplanade, is the **Irish Hunger Memorial** (2002).

Between 1845 and 1852 a recurring blight destroyed the crucial Irish potato crop and led to the starvation death of over a million Irish farmers and the emigration of a million more. Many came to New York, dramatically shifting the city's demographics. By 1850 over a quarter of the city's population was Irish-born.

The impressive memorial's design is the work of Brian Tolle with Gail Wittwer-Laird and the firm 1100 Architect. An elevated quarter-acre concrete platform slopes up toward the river to a height of 25 feet. Its surface

Figure 2.15. Irish Hunger Memorial.

is landscaped to recall a deserted village in County Mayo and includes an actual ruined cottage from the 1820s, shipped to New York from Ireland and re-erected. The landscaping includes rocks from all 32 of Ireland's counties as well as over 60 varieties of native Irish plants. One enters the memorial on the western side through a sleek, sloping trapezoidal corridor leading to the remains of the cottage and to a winding path up through the planted landscape to a viewing platform. Behind the glass panels in the corridor are illuminated quotations—lyrics, poetry, statistics, and other writings—focused both on the Irish Hunger and on the issue of world hunger today. These are supplemented by a spoken-word soundtrack.

The **Conrad New York Hotel** (2000; Perkins Eastman) with its soaring atrium enlivened by a sprawling blue Sol LeWitt mural rises to the east behind the memorial. Towering above the hotel is the cool, sleek curving facade of the **Goldman Sachs Tower** at 200 West Street (2009; Henry N. Cobb of Pei Cobb Freed & Partners). North End Way, a pedestrian street separating the two buildings, is dramatically roofed by a slanting glass canopy that reaches out yearningly from the Goldman Sachs Tower but does not quite reach the hotel.

The northern section of Battery Park City, from Vesey to Chambers Street, has a distinctly different feel from the neighborhoods to the south. Beyond the Hunger Memorial the tourists and office workers vanish, replaced by the residents of what is a decidedly upscale neighborhood. Here tall apartment buildings are set back from the water, separated from the esplanade by the broad green of eight-acre **Rockefeller Park** (1992; Carr, Lynch, Hack & Sandell with Oehme, van Sweden & Associates). It is the largest open space within Battery Park City. Along its eastern edge a curving path passes a lily pond with a small waterfall, an elaborate children's playground, a basketball court, and a raised seating area and sculpture park. Along the way there is a rustic service building and a **pavilion**.

The latter is an intriguing design by Demetri Porphyrios (1991). Rising from a stepped granite plinth, 12 thin wooden columns with copper capitals support a broad flat roof. Inside, on an additional stepped plinth are four more columns, this time thick and massive, constructed of salvaged brick.

Figure 2.16. Pavilion, Rockefeller Park.

Topped with Doric limestone capitals, these columns create a small open interior room—the *cella* of an abstracted Greek temple. Warm and sensuous in its materials, but of limited utility, the structure seems to occupy an ambivalent space between sculpture and architecture.

The sculpture garden at the north end of the park is the work of artist Tom Otterness. His installation, entitled ***The Real World*** (1992), features groupings of cartoonish bronze figures engaging in various pantomime conversations on political and social issues.

The pathway terminates in a substantial granite stairway leading up to Chambers Street by way of a circular terrace. At the top ***My Cry Into the World*** (2021) is a memorial to the victims of Hurricane Maria, which in September 2017 struck the island of Puerto Rico with devastating force. The ascending glass spiral was designed by Segundo Cardona and includes panels painted by Antonio Martorell to evoke both the power of the hurricane and the resiliency of the Puerto Rican community. The poem incorporated into the memorial is by Julia de Burgos.

River Terrace, overlooking the park, is lined with tall brick and glass apartment buildings. By the time these were developed in the late 1990s

Figure 2.17. River Terrace Apartments.

and early 2000s, the initial Battery Park City Authority (BPCA) guidelines had evolved to include sustainability as a priority. These were intended to be among New York's first truly "green" buildings, designed for energy efficiency and indoor environmental quality. Apartments have energy efficient appliances, rooftop gardens, solar panels, gray water collection tanks, and bike storage areas.

River Terrace moves along the top of Rockefeller Park in a sweeping curve, a curve that is echoed in the building's facades. In their relationship to the street, the park, and the river, the grouping deliberately recalls the layout of Riverside Drive on the Upper West Side.

The buildings here are architecturally more ambitious and varied than those to the south. The row begins with **River House** (2009; Polshek Partnership, Ismael Leyva, David Rockwell) between Barclay and Murray Streets, a somewhat busy composition anchored by a southern tower. Next door the **Solaire** at 20 River Terrace (2003; Pelli Clarke Pelli with SLCE Architects) and **22 River Terrace** (2001; Gruzen Samton) are fraternal twins, sharing the massing and materials with River House but exhibiting a slightly more extroverted personality. (Note the solar panels embedded in the facade of the Pelli building.) **Tribeca Park**, 400 Chambers Street (1999; Robert A. M. Stern with Costa Kondylis) is more visually distinctive, even if the detailing is a bit self-conscious and the relationship between the different wings does not always cohere. Finally, towering over the other buildings in the group, and to a certain degree turning its back on them, is the **Tribeca Pointe Tower** at 41 River Terrace (1999; Gruzen Samton). The building's distinctive blue and orange polychrome also sets it apart.

In many ways the most interesting and surprising feature of the River Terrace buildings is what is hidden behind them. **Teardrop Park** (2004; Michael Van Valkenburgh with Ann Hamilton and Michael Mercil) is a 1.8-acre oasis inspired by the landscape of the Catskill Mountains. Surrounded closely on all sides by tall apartment blocks, each of which has a rear entrance opening directly onto the park, Teardrop Park is a dramatic, mysterious landscape of mountains, cliffs, and valleys. Perhaps the most arresting feature is a large diagonal rock wall, 27 feet tall, constructed from bluestone slabs trucked in from upstate New York. They are laid in rising courses that suggest that they were formed—pushed up—by natural forces. Water drips from the rocks as if from natural springs, and icicles form on the wall in winter. The rock wall shields a play space with a long slide, sand pits, an amphitheater, and a water playground. The northern section of the park is accessible through a tunnel piercing the rock wall and is set

Figure 2.18. Teardrop Park.

aside for quieter activities. Everywhere there are hidden places to explore and quiet benches on which to relax.

The large building housing **Stuyvesant High School** marks the northern terminus of Battery Park City. In 1986 the city committed to creating a new home for the prestigious public high school that had long occupied a fine building on East 15th Street. Facing West Street at the extreme northeastern corner of Battery Park City, Stuyvesant (1992; Alexander Cooper & Partners with Gruzen Samton Steinglass) is a major institution, a wedge-shaped building of over 400,000 square feet, serving 2,700 students. Thanks to lobbying by a coalition of students, teachers, parents, and administrators, it includes features and finishes seldom found in contemporary public school buildings.

On the exterior, Stuyvesant High School is an intriguing building. Each of the structure's three visible facades has a distinct personality. The southern wing, facing Chambers Street and housing classrooms, offices, and the library, is formal and symmetrical with a central entry facing down North End Avenue. The northern elevation is far less unified. Three distinct blocks reflect the locations of the gymnasiums, the theater with its postmodern faux pediment, and the art studios. The latter block is topped with a large dining terrace. The eastern facade is similarly articulated into three distinct

Figure 2.19. Chambers Street Bridge.

sections: the side of the gym block, a low entry pavilion with a curved facade, and the end of the main classroom block. The overall effect evokes the syncopated hodgepodge of industrial structures that long dominated this neighborhood.

Since many of Stuyvesant's students arrive from distant neighborhoods, a bridge was erected to allow them to safely cross busy West Street.

Skidmore, Owings & Merrill (1994) went all out, designing a bold white bowstring truss bridge that angles across the highway to connect Chambers Street with the second level of the school. The bridge feels overdesigned, but it fulfills an important secondary function: It is a dramatic marker visually signaling the northern boundary of Battery Park City.

3

Chambers Street to Gansevoort Street

Chambers Street marks the beginning of Tribeca, the fashionable neighborhood whose name is an acronym for Triangle Below Canal. Farther north we will pass through SoHo (South of Houston) and conclude this walk on the edges of Greenwich Village.

Much of the land along the river between Fulton and Christopher Streets was originally the King's Farm, a 215-acre tract owned by Trinity Church. In the early nineteenth century as river traffic shifted from the East River to the Hudson, the neighborhood was developed to support the shipping industry. At the same time, the area just north of Chambers Street became New York's principal marketplace for produce—the Washington Market. It remained active until the 1960s when it was relocated to Hunts Point in the Bronx. The original buildings were demolished in 1964, and part of the site was turned into a city park in 1981.

The section of the waterfront north of Canal Street quickly became among the busiest along the river—packed with piers, warehouses, tenements, saloons, and sailors' hotels. In recent years some former warehouses have been converted into loft apartments. Others have been demolished and replaced with new construction. Favored by celebrities, art galleries, boutiques, and restaurants, today it is one of the city's most exclusive neighborhoods.

In these blocks, West Street, a six-lane divided trafficway running just to the east of the river, is a constant presence. The street's current configuration can be traced to the demolition of the old elevated West Side (Miller) Highway. With the elevated highway gone, the city faced the problem of its replacement. The proposed solution was Westway, which was to become

Figure 3.1. Map 3.

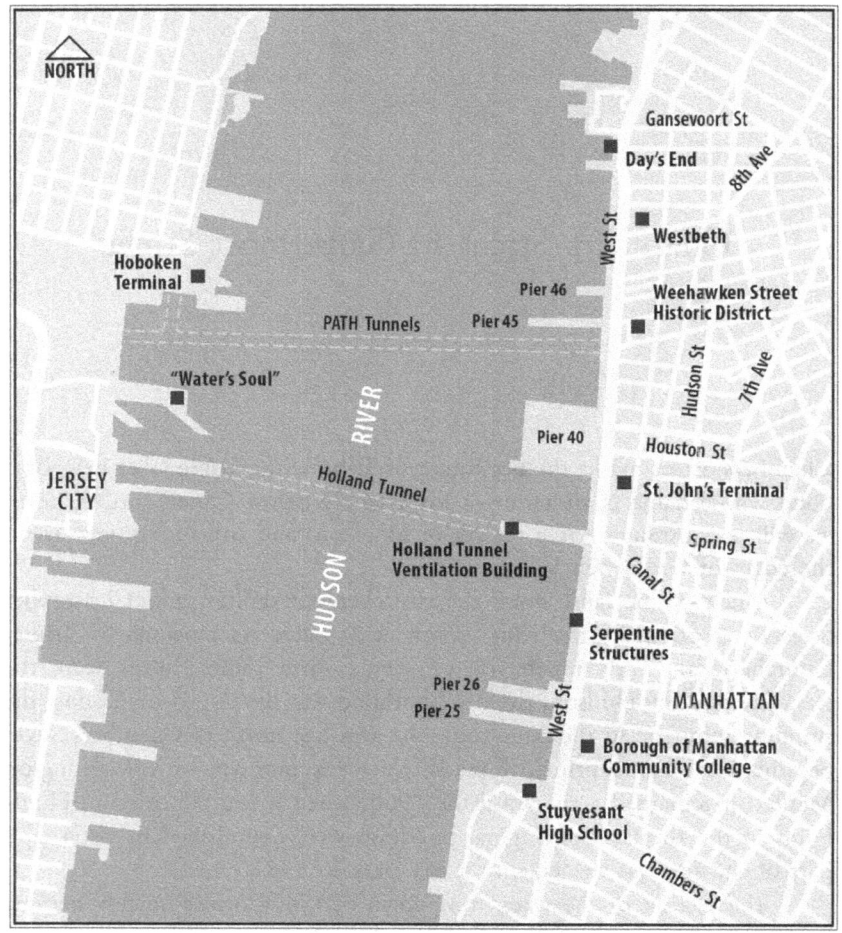

one of the most complex and controversial episodes in the history of New York transportation. Hoping to take advantage of federal infrastructure funds, the city and state proposed to replace the West Side Highway with a new 8-to-10-lane expressway located on the river 100 feet east of the pier line. Opposition to the project was fierce, and numerous alternative proposals were floated, including a six-lane buried highway. Lawsuits and court orders, political deals, and real estate chicanery followed. In the end, a combination of environmental issues and changing visions for life in the city doomed the project; by 1985 it was dead. The $1 billion of the originally allocated federal money was redirected to mass transit projects, and West Street was rebuilt in its current form as a surface highway. The new roadway was ultimately completed in 2001.

In conjunction with the reconstruction of West Street, the state legislature designated the land to the west of the new highway between Chambers and 59th Streets as the **Hudson River Park**. What was a four-mile stretch of postindustrial wasteland and derelict piers is steadily being reclaimed and reanimated. The 1998 Hudson River Park Act established a trust, a public/private partnership, to operate and maintain the new park. Design and construction costs were to be covered by grants from the city, state, and federal governments, supplemented by private contributions. Once built, the park was envisioned as self-sustaining. This proved a challenge until new legislation allowed the trust to sell air rights to developers and to collect rents from businesses on the rebuilt piers within the park. Hudson River Park remains a work in progress but has already brought about a Renaissance to a long stretch of the Hudson waterfront thorough a combination of landscaped walkways, sports fields, playgrounds, fishing and docking facilities, skate parks, kayaking and sailing centers, restaurants, and educational facilities. A paved, two-way bike path runs along the park's western edge, beside busy West Street. The path is a popular component of the Hudson River Greenway, a designated cycling route that extends all the way from Battery Park to Inwood Hill Park at the northern end of Manhattan Island.

Pier 25 is the first, and among the longest piers in the park, extending a full 985 feet into the river. It is home to an 18-hole miniature golf course, as well as sports fields, volleyball courts, and docking spaces for historic ships. At present these include the wooden schooner Sherman Zwicker, which houses a restaurant, and the Lilac, a former Coast Guard buoy tender built in 1933.

Pier 26 just to the north is focused on ecology. It features a compact garden planted with native species, a sunning deck, and a tide deck. This cantilevered walkway, designed like the rest of the pier by the landscape firm OLIN, opened in 2020 and provides access to a newly constructed salt marsh at river level. Environmental educational programs are offered here in partnership with Clarkson University. On shore a new science play area, also designed by OLIN (2023), focuses on the Hudson River's marine habitat. The playground includes a huge metal sturgeon, through which children can climb.

Figure 3.2. Pier 26.

Across West Street the view is dominated by the main campus of the **Borough of Manhattan Community College** (1980–1983; Caudill Rowlett Scott Partnership). This megastructure, loosely inspired by the shape of an ocean liner, spans four full city blocks from Chambers to North Moore Street. Founded in 1963 as a branch of CUNY, the college has additional locations scattered in buildings around midtown. Although this and most of the other buildings on the eastern side of West Street can be best and most safely viewed from Hudson River Park, it is worth a detour across the busy trafficway to the rear of the community college building, where one of the stylish Art Deco cartouches that once marked cross streets on the now dismantled Miller Highway has been preserved on a pedestrian walkway over Harrison Street.

Note that the cartouches, designed by John Sloane of Sloane & Robertson, are labeled not with street names but with pier numbers.

Just to the north opposite Piers 25 and 26 at the corner of West and North Moore Streets stands the 39-story tower originally known as Shearson Lehman Plaza. Today it is the global headquarters of **Citigroup**. The tower (1989; Kohn Pederson Fox) is linked to a shorter building immediately to the north, 390 Greenwich Street (1986; Skidmore, Owings & Merrill). The

Figure 3.3. Cartouche from the West Side Highway.

two buildings—one originally blocky and understated in style, the other more assertively postmodern with a pedimented rooftop temple—were renovated in 2019. A new glass curtain wall was applied to visually unite the two structures, which had long been linked internally.

Continuing north, the huge brick and limestone warehouse at **250 West Street** (1903–1906; William H. Birkmire) has been converted into condos by GNA architects. Next door at **79 Laight Street**, the handsome former home of the Grocers Steam Sugar Refining Company from 1853, is also a condo conversion (2002). It has retained its thick brick walls pierced by regularly spaced and segmentally arched windows with brownstone sills. Original iron fire shutters are in place on the lower two floors, and iron tie rods with star-shaped end plates punctuate the West Street facade.

The next block is occupied by two more residential conversions. **92 Laight Street** is a 2004 condo building by Tsao & McKown. The 13-story tower is linked to an 1882 loft building at 416 Washington Street. The red brick and limestone structure works hard, and with some success, to fit in with its older commercial neighbors. Note the addition of the simulated loading bays under a glass canopy along West and Laight Streets.

Figure 3.4. 79 Laight Street.

67 Vestry Street at the southeast corner of Vestry and West Streets was built in 1897 by architect Frank Dinkelberg as a warehouse for the Great Atlantic and Pacific Tea Company (the A&P). The building was expanded in 1910 by two stories. Long known for its artists' studios (Marisol, John Chamberlin, and Robert Wilson lived and worked here) the pale brick and terracotta palazzo has once again been updated (2022; BP Architects) including the addition of a large penthouse.

70 Vestry Street (2018; RAMSA), filling the full block between Vestry and Desbrosses Streets, is a characteristically balanced and dignified Robert Stern composition clad in French limestone.

450 Washington Street, between Desbrosses and Watts, is a 2022 update by Roger Ferris + Partners. The original blocky, concrete building, picturesquely dubbed Truffles Tribeca, dates to 2009 and was the work of Handel Architects.

456 Washington Street at the northeast corner of West and Watts Streets is a large rental apartment building extending the full block east to Washington Street. Like many buildings in these blocks, the 2016 structure by BKSK Architects seems to turn its back to the river, presenting a bland face to West Street. Whenever possible, developers in this neighborhood choose to provide their buildings with addresses and entries on Washington Street or on east–west side streets rather than on busy and noisy West Street, even though it is the views over the river that give the properties their caché.

Next door, **288 West Street** has long been known as the Medium Lipstick Building. It was built as a spice warehouse in the 1860s. While the origins of the building's name remain obscure—maybe the color of the brick?—the structure is a handsome one despite the blank, staring single

Figure 3.5. The "Medium Lipstick Building."

pane windows that have replaced the mullioned originals. The fine arched twin portals remain intact.

290 West Street at the southeast corner of West and Canal Streets completes the block. Here the industrial glass facade is segmented into a neat grid by metal channels that suggest I-beams. Only at the penthouse level does a single projecting bay break the contained cubic geometry.

To the west, the Hudson River Park walkway between Piers 26 and 34 is bordered by nicely planted beds and lawns demarcated by what seem to be randomly placed stone walls and planting beds. On the landward side, a meandering raised wooden walkway threads its way through a landscape of shoreline grasses and red cedars. The slightly elevated landscaped berms work to shield the riverside esplanade from the noise and traffic of West Street. The overall design is the work of Mathews Nielsen Landscape Architects.

This section of Hudson River Park is also home to a series of industrial truss sculptures by Marc Gibian. The three complex ***Serpentine Structures*** (2008)—Offshoot, Torque, and Twister—are constructed of welded steel pipe and inspired by estuarian marine life. Their visually arresting forms neatly straddle the line between art and engineering. It is also worth keeping your eye on the pavement along this stretch of the esplanade. Occasionally surprises appear, such as a pair of small bronze pavers engraved with a poem by Senegalese writer and diplomat Birago Diop.

At regular intervals along the riverfront esplanade, granite posts indicate the numbers of vanished piers. At the site of **Pier 32** the river still contains a forest of truncated wooden pilings, left in place to provide a welcoming habitat for marine life.

Pier 34 juts out into the Hudson at Canal Street. Unlike its companions to the south, it is not a thematically programmed space. The pier's raison d'être can be found at the western end of its two long parallel fingers: a ventilation building for the Holland Tunnel.

The tunnel was the first vehicular crossing of the Hudson, a 1.6-mile engineering marvel that opened for traffic in November of 1927. Construction took seven years, and at the time of its opening it was the longest such tunnel in the world.

Before its construction, automobiles and freight-carrying trucks could only cross the river by barge or ferry, a slow and laborious process. As river traffic increased, the Hudson was often dangerously clogged with boats. In response a commission was appointed to study the construction of a road link between New Jersey and Manhattan. Two competing proposals emerged: a bridge at 57th Street and a tunnel at Canal Street. Cost projections and

Figure 3.6. Holland Tunnel ventilation building.

the intervention of the War Department, concerned about the vulnerability of bridges, swung the balance in favor of the tunnel.

Because of the proposed tunnel's length, designers could not rely on natural air flow to remove automotive exhaust from the tubes, so they designed a mechanical system to do the work. Four massive ventilation towers, one in Manhattan at Canal and Washington Street, a second near the tunnel's western end in Jersey City, and two additional towers on piers set out over the river, contain 84 gigantic fans that exhaust stale air and pump in fresh. The ventilation buildings themselves, designed by tunnel engineer Clifford Holland (for whom the tunnel is named) and architect Erling Owre, are an attractive blend of form and function. Monumental in scale and solid in form, they are sleek and modern in style. We will encounter similar ventilations buildings, also designed by Owre, farther north at the Lincoln Tunnel.

The Holland Tunnel is one of three Hudson crossings managed by the Port Authority of New York and New Jersey. The Hudson, of course, marks the boundary between two states; and from colonial days forward the issue of who would control commerce along and across the river had been a contentious one. Finally, in 1921 a compact between the two states was signed creating a special body with broad authority to manage and develop both the port and interstate river crossings. Over the years, the Port Authority has assumed control of all bridges and vehicular tunnels connecting New York City and New Jersey as well as of three regional airports, the PATH train line, two Manhattan bus terminals, and a major container port on the New Jersey side.

Just across West Street from Pier 34 in front of the eastern tunnel ventilation building stands the **Spring Street Salt Shed**, a remarkably dramatic and sculptural solution to a mundane sanitation problem: where to store the mountains of salt needed to keep Manhattan's streets clear of winter ice. The shed (2015; Dattner Architects with WXY Architecture + Urban Design) is constructed of faceted cast-in-place concrete panels six feet thick and rising nearly 70 feet from the pavement. The shed can store 5,000 tons of salt. Depending on which account one favors, the building's

Figure 3.7. Spring Street salt shed.

powerful geometries were inspired either by the crystalline form of the salt it contains or by a crumpled piece of paper. Built in the face of significant initial opposition from the area's wealthy residents, the shed has become a much admired work of urban sculpture.

The same architects are responsible for the neighboring **Manhattan 1/2/5 Garage** immediately to the north, designed to house and service 150 garbage trucks from across the borough. The upper floors of the huge 425,000-square-foot building rise above a brick setback at ground level. Each of the upper floors is color coded by its Manhattan sanitation district. Thanks to a double skin, a glass curtain wall, and a layer of perforated metal fins to diffuse glare and reduce heat gain, the massive building has a surprising lightness. The two structures, the garage and salt shed, play off against each other beautifully—transparency versus solidity, simple right angles versus complex abstract geometries.

The sanitation buildings stand at the foot of **Canal Street**, named for the drainage ditch that long directed water from the Collect Pond just north of City Hall into the Hudson River. Canal Street forms the southern boundary of the Hudson Square neighborhood, a locale once famous as a center of the printing trades. Much of the land in the vicinity is still owned by Trinity Church, and following rezoning in 2013 it has been redeveloped by such major corporations as Disney and Google.

Just to the north of the sanitation complex is the **St. John's Terminal**, erected in 1934 as the southern terminus of the New York Central Railway's High Line. The original terminal was a massive low-lying structure that could accommodate 227 freight cars. With the end of rail service in 1960, the building was converted to warehouse and office use. It was acquired by Google in 2021 and is being expanded as a part of the company's growing campus in the neighborhood, the so-called Googleplex. Google was able to add a nine-story addition thanks to the unusually large foundations already in place to support the train cars and through the transfer of 200,000 square feet of air rights from nearby Pier 40. The sale of these rights provided vital income to the then-struggling Hudson River Park. The designers of the expansion, COOKFOX Architects, have worked to keep the height of the expanded building in line with other structures in the neighborhood and on the north facade have even retained some reminders of the terminal's history: The concrete stubs of the original train platforms can clearly be seen.

Walking north along the river it is hard to miss the south-facing side of Pier 40 where the words I WANT TO THANK YOU are boldly painted in red. The mural is the work of artist Stephen Powers, inspired by

Figure 3.8. St. John's Terminal.

lyrics in a song by Alicia Meyers. Executed in 2019, the work was part of a campaign to encourage support of The Global Fund, a charity supporting research and treatment of HIV, tuberculosis, and malaria.

Pier 40 itself owes its existence to a late burst of maritime optimism. Despite evidence that transatlantic air service was quickly bringing the great age of ocean liners to an end, in 1958 the City of New York demolished five aging wharfs and erected a huge new passenger pier. It opened in 1962 as the home of the Holland America Line, lured across the river from its longtime base in Hoboken. The new pier was at the time the largest and most modern passenger and freight terminal on the river and served Holland America until 1974 when the line moved its operations to the New York Passenger Ship Terminal farther uptown. In 1998 Pier 40 was incorporated into Hudson River Park, but artist Frank Nix's large ceramic mural celebrating the Holland American Line is still in place in the main entrance lobby. Today the 14.5-acre pier is a major sports center.

The pier is essentially a square donut. At its center is a vast turf field, accommodating soccer pitches, baseball diamonds, and the home field of the New York Knights rugby team. A large parking garage occupies much of the surrounding building. The pier is also home to the offices of the

Figure 3.9. Pier 40. *Source:* Alamy.

Hudson River Park Trust; the Wetlab, an aquarium and marine biology field station; docking facilities for tour boats; and up on the roof, a trapeze school. Income from parking and sports activities at Pier 40 today generates 40 percent of the Hudson River Park's operating budget. As a telling indicator of how dramatically the city's vision for this stretch of the waterfront has evolved, it is worth noting that in the mid-1980s local residents fought off a proposal to anchor a pair of huge prison barges at Pier 40.

The vacant lot just across West Street from the pier is currently under development—the site for a 36-story super-luxury condo to be designed by COOKFOX.

Next door, to the north of the development site, the rounded pavilions of **160 Leroy Street** (2017; Herzog & de Meuron with Ian Schrager) fill the full block along West Street between Clarkson and Leroy. Right angles are in short supply here as the architects worked, in the words of the developer, to achieve a design that is "curvaceous, sensual, free flowing, seductive, and sexy." The building, with its faceted floor-to-ceiling windows and crisp concrete facade, is eye-catching and luxurious even if it would be more at home in Miami Beach than Manhattan. The entrance is at the rear, off a private garden that provides comfort to those whose apartments lack a river view.

Figure 3.10. 160 Leroy Street and Morton Square.

There are more curves in evidence in the following block. **Morton Square**, occupying the full block between Leroy and Morton Streets, is a mundane condo and rental building completed in 2004 by Costas Kondylis & Partners. Things are more architecturally interesting across West Street. Two geometrically patterned towers stand in Hudson River Park at the foot of Morton Street. Their style is vaguely Vienna Secession, but their purpose is to provide emergency access and ventilation for a second northern set of **PATH tunnels** under the Hudson. Beginning in Jersey City, these tunnels enter Manhattan here before continuing onward to Christopher Street and then uptown under Sixth Avenue to a final terminus at 33rd Street. Original plans called for a further extension to Grand Central Terminal, but this was never completed. Unlike the nearby Holland Tunnel, which required mechanical ventilation, the PATH tunnels are self-ventilating. The electric train cars passing through the narrow tubes create a vacuum, drawing in fresh air.

The landmarked **Keller Hotel** stands at the corner of Barrow and West Streets. Opened in 1898, the Renaissance-style building is the work of Julius Munckwitz, the longtime supervising architect of the New York parks system. The building, constructed of brick with dignified stone detailing and a prominent cornice, was built to accommodate both travelers and workers in what was by the turn of the twentieth century the busiest section of the New York waterfront. In later years as the activity at the docks declined, it became a single-room-occupancy welfare hotel. The building is currently being converted to apartments. The Keller is among the last survivors from an era when similar waterfront hotels once filled the blocks along West Street. The ground floor space at the corner of West and Barrow was for a number of years the home of a well-known bar catering to a gay clientele. Across the way in the park at the foot of Christopher Street, the **Marshal P. Johnson Memorial Fountain** honors the prominent gay rights activist and drag queen.

The corner of Christopher and West Streets marks the beginning of the tiny 14-building **Weehawken Street Historic District**. The district presents a chronological cross section of the development of buildings along the Hudson waterfront from the 1830s onward. These buildings replaced the area's first occupant, New York's Newgate Prison (active from 1796 to 1828). The prison was succeeded by a range of maritime businesses, saloons, and a market. The unprepossessing shingled frame structure at **392–393 West Street** dates back to 1834 and is the sole remaining, although much altered, section of the original market building.

The **Holland Hotel** at 396–397 West Street has more architectural character. Built in 1904 to designs by Charles Stegmayer, the hotel was constructed of buff brick, now painted red. A spirited oriel supported by a slender cast iron column anchors the corner of West 10th Street.

Back in Hudson River Park, **Pier 45** stretches a full 900 feet out into the Hudson. To prevent long ships from extending beyond the end of the pier into the channel, a semicircular cut was made in the bulkhead. It can still be seen just to the north of the pier. In 1807 Robert Fulton's *Clermont*, the first steam powered passenger vessel in America, was launched from this spot. The *Clermont* began a new era in navigation on the river and was the precursor of the great transatlantic passenger vessels whose piers once lined this stretch of the Hudson waterfront. Today the main attractions of Pier 45 are its broad grassy lawn and the pavilion at the western end—the site of popular Sunset Salsa dance gatherings.

Pier 45 is a convenient place from which to look across the river to the **Hoboken Terminal**. The first steam ferries crossing the Hudson began

Figure 3.11. Holland Hotel.

service here in 1811. The present terminal was built in 1907 for the Delaware, Lackawanna, and Western Railway to designs by the prolific railway station architect Kenneth Murchison. The railroad's ferries continued to operate from Hoboken to Barclay Street until 1967. After a hiatus, ferry service returned in 1987. Today the station is a key nexus for New Jersey Transit commuter trains, PATH trains, local buses, and the Hudson–Bergen Light Rail Line. The richly embellished Beaux Arts–style building is clad from top to bottom in beautifully oxidized copper and marked by a dramatic clock tower, a reconstruction of the lost original. Of the five major railway terminals that once populated the New Jersey shore of the Hudson, the Hoboken Terminal is the only one still in active use.

Just to the south of the terminal at the tip of the next pier on the Jersey shore is **Water's Soul**, a colossal gleaming white fiberglass female head by Spanish artist Jaime Plensa. It was commissioned as part of the redevelopment of the Newport neighborhood of Jersey City.

Figure 3.12. Hoboken Terminal.

On the Manhattan side, **Pier 46** is a junior partner to the longer Pier 45. Here only the inner section of the pier was reconstructed. The outline of its original extent can be seen by the pile field remaining in the river.

Pier 46 provides a good view of three cool, glossy 15-story glass towers designed by Richard Meier just across West Street to the east. The two northern buildings at **173 and 176 Perry Street** went up first in 2002.

Each floor was designed as a single loft-like apartment. (There is also a dramatic 11-room triplex penthouse at the top of 176.) Each has a south-facing balcony shielded by frosted glass. The floor-to-ceiling glazing of the interior rooms is set back behind a grid of steel beams. Access is at the east side of the buildings through a dramatically contrasting concrete stair/elevator tower.

Following the success of the two Perry Street buildings, Meier designed a third to the south in 2006. At **165 Charles Street** the balconies are inset, and the frosted glass is gone. The overall effect is sleeker, more planar, and less aggressively gridded. The elevator tower here is incorporated into the main block where there are two apartments on each floor, all designed by the architect. Note the whimsical wooden "tree house" constructed inside the combined apartments on the lower two residential floors. It is the work of architect Andrew Heid.

Imitation is said to be the highest form of flattery. As an illustration, consider **423 West Street**, a rental building erected in 2005 by Patrick Han/ HB2 Architects just north of the Meier towers.

The **Bell Telephone Laboratories/Westbeth Artists' Housing** is a five-building complex filling the entire square block along West Street between Bank and Bethune Streets. The original structures, at 445-453 West Street,

Figure 3.13. 173 and 176 Perry St. and 165 Charles St.

were erected ca. 1860 as Hook's Steam Powered Factory. This is one of the oldest surviving groups of industrial buildings on the waterfront. Between 1896 and 1903 Cyrus Eidlitz designed a series of connected buff-colored brick and terracotta buildings to the north of the Steam Factory along West Street and eastward on Bethune Street for the Western Electric Company, which manufactured equipment for the Bell Telephone system. The complex was gradually expanded by other designers to fill the entire block. By 1925 manufacturing ceased, and the buildings became home to the Bell Telephone Laboratories. In its prime Eidlitz's handsome classically designed building was the site of breakthrough research that saw the production of the first vacuum tube amplifier, the first condenser microphone, and the first system for synchronized sound for motion pictures. Other pioneering work here led to the development of LP records, television, and the first digital computer. Space constraints along with increased noise from truck and rail traffic, led to the relocation of the labs to Murray Hill, New Jersey in 1941.

Bell moved out completely in 1966, and with the sponsorship of the National Endowment for the Arts and the J. M. Kaplan Fund the buildings were converted into 384 subsidized studio and duplex apartments for working artists, writers, and performers. There are also gallery, performance, and

Figure 3.14. Westbeth.

commercial spaces in the building. The conversion (completed in 1970) was the first major work of architect Richard Meier, inspired by the example of Swiss architect Le Corbusier's Unité d'Habitation in Marseilles. Westbeth is a pioneering example of adaptive reuse and marked a significant step toward zoning changes that would allow industrial buildings and lofts elsewhere in the city to be converted into living and studio spaces. The creation of the complex also marked a turning point for this section of the then seriously declined Hudson waterfront, pointing the way to its reemergence as a desirable residential neighborhood.

The block just to the north of Westbeth was for years the site of a large industrial building erected in 1919 by Nabisco. It later became the home of the Superior Ink Company. The old building did not survive, but Robert Stern adopted the design of its lower floors for his condominium tower at 400 West 12th Street. He kept the name too. The new Superior

Ink condo building (2009) in its symmetry, traditional materials, and careful proportions is recognizably Stern. The complex includes not just the main tower but a row of seven townhouses along Bethune Street.

495 West Street (1999; Cary Tamarkin and Schuman, Lichtenstein, Claman & Efron) cheerfully embraces the neighborhood's industrial heritage and adds a touch of Art Deco. Its most dramatic feature is the lushly planted terrace that introduces a large penthouse.

This stretch of West Street concludes with the picturesque **American Seamen's Friend Society Sailors' Home and Institute** at the northwest corner of Jane Street (1907–1908). The neoclassical brick and cast stone building with its eye-catching polygonal tower and nautical themed decorative motifs is the work of architect William A. Boring, best known for his immigration complex on Ellis Island. The Seamen's Friend Society was founded in 1828 as a religious organization dedicated to improving "the social, moral and religious condition of seamen; to protect them from imposition and fraud; to prevent them from becoming a curse to each other

Figure 3.15. Seamen's Friend Society building.

and the world; to rescue them from sin and its consequences, and to save their souls . . . [and] to sanctify commerce, an interest and a power in the earth, second only to religion itself."

The New York branch of the society was originally located on the East River, but as the center of the New York waterfront shifted to the Hudson, it moved to this site. The society operated as a home for indigent sailors and offered not just lodging in 156 cabin-like rooms, but an auditorium, dining rooms, a chapel, library, swimming pool, laundry, and clothing store. It was here that the surviving crew members from the *Titanic* found refuge. The society eventually sold its building to the YMCA, which continued to operate here until 1946 when, to signal the end of the building's original mission, the lighthouse/observatory that long topped the tower was removed. In more recent times, as the Riverview and then as the Jane Hotel, the building attracted a celebrity crowd to events in its ballroom nightclub. The hotel is now in the process of being converted into a private club.

The section of **Hudson River Park** between Piers 45 and 51 was the first to be completed (2002) and the plantings in the upland between the riverside walkway and West Street are now mature. Note in particular those around Charles Street in the Apple Garden centered on a bronze sculpture (2004) by Stephen Weiss. This section of the park also contains two major memorials. Anthony Goicolea's LGBT Memorial is located between Bethune and West 12th Streets. The memorial (2018) is dedicated to those who lost their lives in the 2016 Orlando Pulse Nightclub shooting, but it also celebrates the larger LGBTQ+ community. Nine bronze "boulders" are arranged in a grove. Some are bisected with sheets of laminated glass that act as a prism to reflect and refract light.

The **AIDS Memorial** is located on a grassy lawn near Bank Street. Dedicated in 2008, the memorial is a 42-foot-long granite bench engraved with text from a Scandinavian folk song: "I can sail without wind, I can row without oars, but I cannot part from my friend without tears."

To the north, at the site of what was Pier 52, David Hammons's ***Day's End*** (2014–2021) is the largest work of public art in the park. The steel outlines trace the silhouette of a lost pier, long a popular gathering place for the gay community. The sculpture, inspired by an earlier work with the same title (1975) on the same site by Gordon Matta-Clark, was a gift to Hudson River Park from the Whitney Museum. Hammons's work is an effective fusion of architecture, sculpture, drawing, and land art whose meaning is enriched by the history and associations of its site. *Day's End* sits at the southern end of the Gansevoort Peninsula, discussed in chapter 4.

Figure 3.16. *Day's End.*

4

Gansevoort Street to the Javits Center

The blocks along the river between Horatio and 15th Streets today constitute the **Gansevoort Market Historic District**, popularly known as the Meatpacking District. Beginning in the 1840s the neighborhood developed as a mix of residences, factories, and commercial buildings. A major change occurred in 1879 when the city opened a municipal produce market here to supplement the old Washington Market downtown.

Between 1897 and 1935 the entire block facing West Street between Horatio and Gansevoort Streets was rebuilt to designs by Lansing Holden, J. Graham Glover, and John B. Snook as cold-storage warehouses. The required cooling plant was designed with sufficient capacity to allow the distribution of refrigerant through a network of underground pipes to multiple warehouses in the neighborhood. The ready availability of cold-storage facilities quickly led to the development of the Gansevoort Market into a major meatpacking center. The opening of the Holland Tunnel (1927), Miller Highway (1931), and High Line (1934) provided essential transportation links that further secured the market's place as New York's principal distribution center for meat and poultry. The market enjoyed thriving business until the 1960s. Today, only a tiny number of meat distributors remain. The neighborhood, thanks in large part to the construction of a new home for the Whitney Museum and the opening of the High Line Park, has been handsomely redeveloped as a center for high-end retail, restaurants, galleries, and apartments.

The history of the **High Line** begins in 1846 when the Hudson River Railroad was granted permission to run tracks down the center of 10th and 11th Avenues to offer a direct freight connection to nearby piers. The line

Figure 4.1. Map 4.

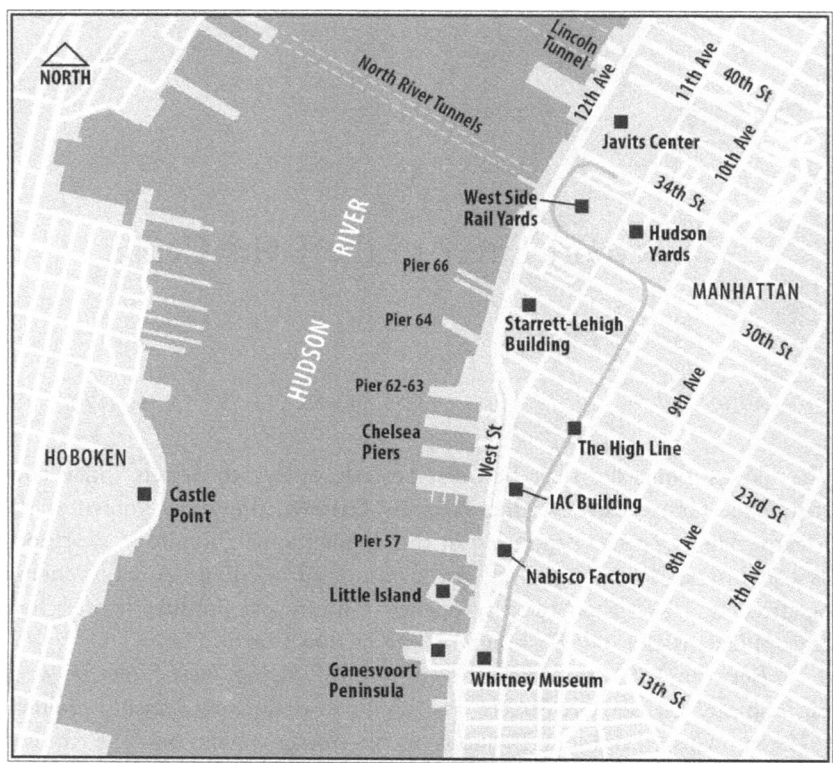

was dangerous from the start; collisions and injuries were frequent. By the early twentieth century, despite the efforts of special mounted police—the "West Side Cowboys"—to clear a path for the trains, over 450 people had lost their lives in railway accidents. Steadily increasing heavy truck traffic made the situation even worse, leading to near gridlock.

As a solution Manhattan Borough President Julius Miller proposed the construction of a double-deck elevated roadway to carry both rail and truck traffic above the congested streets. In the end, two roughly parallel structures were built—one for vehicular traffic, one for rail. After multiple construction delays, the New York Central's West Side Elevated Line finally opened for service in 1934. Running on a trestle south from the freight yards west of Penn Station to the new St. John's Terminal at Houston Street, the rail line's tracks passed directly through the second floor of 30 buildings where freight could be loaded and unloaded. By the 1960s, however, traffic along the line had significantly declined, and the section south of Gansevoort Street was demolished. The full line closed in the 1980s; decay began, and there were frequent calls for demolition of what was seen as an eyesore. In 1999 an advocacy group, the Friends of the High Line, was formed to lobby for the preservation of the structure as a public park.

By the early 2000s zoning changes to allow the conversion were in place. The CSX railway, which had inherited the line, donated ownership to the city. Architects James Corner Field Operations, Diller Scofidio + Renfro, and Piet Oudolf were engaged to design the new park. The first section from Gansevoort to 20th Street opened in 2009. In subsequent years additional segments were added, and by 2019 the full 1.45-mile landscaped greenway from Gansevoort to 30th Street was open.

More recently connections have been added to link the High Line directly to the Hudson Yards development and, via a new trestle, all the way to the Moynihan Train Hall at Penn Station.

Figure 4.2. The High Line. *Source:* Alamy.

Today the High Line is one of the city's most popular and loved attractions, beautifully planted with native species and punctuated with gardens and public art installations. City owned, but privately operated and programmed, the High Line has become a national model for the conversion of abandoned railway corridors into public parks and amenities.

If the creation of the High Line park was a key factor in the rejuvenation of neighborhoods along its route, the opening of a new home for the **Whitney Museum of American Art** (2011–2015; Renzo Piano Building Workshop) secured the Gansevoort Market's reputation as one of Manhattan's most lively and trendy districts.

Founded in 1930 by Gertrude Vanderbilt Whitney on Eighth Street in Greenwich Village, the Whitney Museum for three decades occupied a formidable Marcel Breuer building uptown on Madison Avenue and 75th Street. Out of space and with meaningful expansion on its existing site a virtual impossibility, the museum made the bold decision to relocate once again downtown.

Figure 4.3. Whitney Museum.

Renzo Piano's design for the Whitney's new home seems at first glance awkward and ungainly. The building appears to have been assembled from a stack of unrelated parts. As one looks more closely, however, there is much to admire: a dramatically cantilevered plaza over the entry, broad sculpture terraces linked through an elegant and complex composition of interlocking steel stairs, and on the facade an artful interplay of glass and steel paneling. Even the mechanical units on the roof have been enlisted to participate in the composition. Piano's design fully embraces the commercial history of the neighborhood, the adjacent stub of the High Line, and the building's prominent location overlooking the Hudson. Indeed, the panoramic vistas of the river from the main gallery on the fifth floor and those to the east from the stacked terraces on the opposite side of the building provide stiff competition for the art on view in the loft-like galleries. It's a fascinating and paradoxically elegant building that gets better the longer one looks at it.

Just to the north of the Whitney Museum is the low-lying home of Interstate Foods, one of the few meat dealers remaining from the heyday of the Gansevoort Market. Looming above, the prominent **Standard Hotel** (2009; Ennead Architects) is composed of two hinged slabs raised 57 feet

Figure 4.4. Standard Hotel.

above the street to straddle the High Line. The dramatic and sculptural composition was designed to provide guests with appealing vistas to the north and south and, not accidentally, views into the hotel rooms from the High Line walkway below.

The **Solar Carve Tower** (2019; Studio Gang) at 40 10th Avenue presents a sleek flat glass facade to the avenue. Its other elevations are more complex, enlivened with tilted diamond-shaped glass facets designed to minimize solar gain to interior offices while simultaneously ensuring that the views west from the High Line are not blocked by the building's envelope.

Just opposite the Whitney Museum, West Street angles slightly to the east to follow 11th Avenue. This marks the place where the Commissioner's 1811 plan for the development of Manhattan begins, replacing the haphazard street arrangement that characterizes the lower part of the island with a rigid grid. It is also the location of some interesting interventions along the Hudson shoreline. By 1837, land in this fast-growing industrial and residential neighborhood was at a premium. To create space for additional development the city undertook a major landfill project. Water lots in the river between 11th and 29th Streets were filled to create a new 13th Avenue on Manhattan's west side and to provide space for new docks.

Difficulties, however, lay ahead. Transatlantic ships continued to grow larger, and by the turn of the twentieth century some liners exceeded 800 feet in length. This required longer piers. But the federal government, which controlled the river beyond the old 400-foot pier line, refused to allow new construction farther into the river, fearing that the channel would be obstructed. The city's only choice was to remove the landfill it had placed in the river, moving the shoreline back to the east to create the needed space for new and longer piers. This "rewatering" is reflected in the eastward swing of West Street in these blocks.

Only one section of the old landfill in the neighborhood was left in place. It became known as the **Gansevoort Peninsula** and was for years used by the city's sanitation department. The peninsula has now been redeveloped as a component of Hudson River Park to designs by James Corner Field Operations. The popular new 5.5-acre peninsula park includes a salt marsh, playing fields, a kayak and small boat launching area, and the Hudson's first sand beach, positioned adjacent to David Hammons's *Day's End*. Alas, water quality is not yet good enough to permit swimming. The eye-catching home of **FDNY's Marine 1** division (2011; CR Studio), an intriguingly sliced geometric form with syncopated fenestration, sits on its own pier at the north end of the Peninsula.

Figure 4.5. Gansevoort Peninsula beach.

The Cunard Line was one of the steamship companies that utilized the new piers built just north of the Gansevoort Peninsula. Between 1911 and 1935 its home base was the now vanished **Pier 54**. It was here that survivors from the sinking of the *Titanic* arrived via the RMS *Carpathia* on April 18 of 1912. (The *Titanic* itself was scheduled to dock at the White Star Lines' Pier 59 nearby.) And it was also from here that the doomed liner Lusitania sailed in May 1915. (Note the miniature models of Cunard ships in the cases along the walkway.) In 1991 after decades of disuse Pier 54 was partly demolished, leaving in place the ghostly steel arch of its former entrance.

In the wake of Hurricane Sandy in 2012, which further damaged what remained of the pier, philanthropist Barry Diller stepped forward with a proposal to replace the ruins with a 2.4-acre park dubbed **Little Island.**

The design of the project was entrusted to Thomas Heatherwick, who sank 280 distinctive tulip-shaped concrete piles of different lengths into the river to support a lushly planted undulating landscape (designed by MNLA) interspersed with dining and performance spaces to create "an immersive experience of nature and art."

Figure 4.6. Little Island. *Source:* Alamy.

Following several environmental lawsuits and a significant infusion of city and state funds, Little Island opened with great fanfare in 2021 as a part of Hudson River Park. While skeptics point to excessive cost overruns for the project (the budget eventually exceeded $260 million), Little Island continues to draw large crowds to explore the planted landscape and the ambitious performance program.

Just to the north, **Pier 57** at 15th Street opened in 1954 as a replacement for an earlier structure (long leased to the Grace Line) that had suffered a major fire. Built not on piles but on concrete caissons, the pier was touted as the world's most modern at the time of its completion. The caissons, measuring up to 360 by 127 by 33 feet, are based on the floating harbors created off the Normandy coast during World War II.

The Grace Line departed in 1967, and the pier was subsequently used for bus storage and as a temporary detention center for protestors during the 2004 Republican National Convention. Five years later, the pier became a part of Hudson River Park, which continues to restore and redevelop it as both a park and as an income producing property. Google is a major tenant, as is City Winery. There is a large food hall and there are plans to lease space inside the submerged caissons themselves. For many, the key attraction is a beautiful two-acre rooftop park and event pavilion, cleverly landscaped and offering stunning views. Handel Architects, the designers, have been careful to retain the original 1950s brick street facade and the distinctive, green-tinted curtain wall of the pier itself.

Figure 4.7. Rooftop park, Pier 57.

To the east, Google also occupies space in the large red brick structure at **85 10th Avenue,** originally built in 1913 as a bakery for Nabisco. The tech giant is also the owner of another Nabisco factory (birthplace of the Oreo and now the home of the Chelsea Market) in the next block to the east. The former Port Authority building, filling the entire block between Eighth and Ninth Avenues north of 15th Street, is yet another Google property.

The **One High Line** condominiums (2016–2022; Bjarke Ingels Group) at 500 West 18th Street are hard to miss. Both the main 36-story tower and its skybridge-linked 26-story companion are clad in gleaming travertine. The towers tilt and twist as they rise theatrically to offer residents river views and to attract the intrigued gaze of passersby.

In terms of architectural ambition, Frank Gehry's **IAC Building** (2004–2007) at 555 West 18th Street gives One High Line a run for its money. This was Gehry's first building in New York. His client was Barry Diller, the backer of Little Island and head of the IAC conglomerate. The result is a 10-story building designed in two stacked sections, both sheathed in bands of clear and dotted glass. The lower floors are blocky and resemble pleated fabric. On the upper tier, set back behind a terrace, the twisting forms of the building are more emphatic and take on the appearance, at least when seen from the west, of a clipper ship propelled by billowing

Figure 4.8. IAC Building.

sails. The entrances are hidden on the side streets to avoid interrupting the building's sleek frosted skin. It's worth stopping by at night when the lights inside make the building translucent instead of reflective. Don't miss the lobby with its dramatic curving wood benches and 118-foot video wall.

High style architecture continues on the north side of 19th Street. **100 11th Avenue** (2007–2010; Jean Nouvel) sports an eye-catching mosaic-like facade composed of 32 different-sized windows, each canted at an angle. Within their aluminum frames each window is tinted in one of three shades, compounding what is already a wildly complex composition. The main block of the building curves around the corner of 11th Avenue and 19th Street for its entire 23-story height, offering tenants views to the south and west. On the seven lower floors a freestanding, semitransparent curtain wall is set forward from the main block to hold the street line. The space between the curtain and building becomes a narrow atrium.

Next door, 550 West 20th Street (1931; Shreve Lamb & Harmon) was originally designed as the **Seamen's House YMCA** to provide housing for merchant sailors. In 1974 it was converted to a women's prison, the Bayview Correctional Facility. The prison was closed in the wake of damage from Hurricane Sandy and plans were developed to convert the structure into a home for organizations supporting the women's rights movement. These plans were abandoned, and the facility is currently slated for development as supportive housing for the homeless. The structure itself is a stripped down, no-nonsense Art Deco composition with crisp brick geometries and a handsome chamfered corner entry that still features the YMCA logo and inlaid nautical motifs.

A block north, **551 West 21st Street** (2015; Foster & Partners) is another high-end condo by an international celebrity architect. The building rises from a four-story base cut with deep recesses. Up above is a precast concrete grid enlivened by inset bronze detailing and panes of colored glass that add welcome warmth to an otherwise chilly composition.

Back on the riverfront, architectural one-upmanship gives way to the huge **Chelsea Piers**. The four piers that today make up the sprawling Chelsea Piers Sports Complex are the largest remaining segment of a major maritime upgrade undertaken by the city, beginning in 1902, to accommodate increasingly large transatlantic liners. Much of the filled land in the neighborhood was owned either by Clement Clarke Moore (author of *A Visit from St. Nicholas*) or the General Theological Seminary. Both owners profited handsomely from the city's decision to purchase back significant portions of the land for rewatering. After landfill was removed at 16th Street the new bulkhead line was a full 560 feet east of the previous one, providing docking space for ships up to 880 feet in length.

To provide a public face to the new piers, the architectural firm of Warren & Wetmore, celebrated for its design of Grand Central Terminal,

Figure 4.9. Chelsea Piers, ca. 1910. *Source:* Alamy.

was engaged to design a handsome unified Beaux Arts headhouse in pink granite stretching between 12th and 22nd Streets.

As we have seen, the southern section of the complex, from the Gansevoort Peninsula to Pier 59, has vanished or been redeveloped. Only this northern portion of the complex remains.

The new piers served ships from the Cunard, White Star, Grace, and American Lines until the mid-1930s when the arrival of new and even longer ships like the French Line's *Normandie* and Cunard's *Queen Mary* exceeded their capacity. New docks for these 1000-foot monsters were constructed farther north, and the Chelsea Piers were relegated to serving cargo vessels. Maritime use effectively ended in the late 1960s, and the piers languished as parking lots and as New York City's automobile tow pound. After surviving proposed demolition to make way for the aborted Westway Project, redevelopment of the site as an entertainment and sports complex began in 1992. Today the remaining piers are home to two ice rinks, an Olympic-sized swimming pool, a field house and track, a rock-climbing wall, a golf driving range, a bowling alley, and docking facilities for private and tour boats. The headhouses are the home to Manhattan's largest television and film production facility. The well-known series *Law and Order* was filmed there. The piers are a lively place, but one deeply regrets that the handsome Warren & Wetmore facades are gone, replaced by tinny siding and giant advertisements.

The pier complex takes its name from the neighborhood immediately to the east. In the mid-eighteenth century, much of the land here was owned by a British military officer, Thomas Clarke, who named his property **Chelsea** after the Royal Army Hospital in London. The Clarke family originally developed their estate as an upscale residential neighborhood. By the time of the Civil War, however, the western blocks near the river were thoroughly industrialized. In recent years, and particularly after the conversion of the High Line to a park, western Chelsea has become fashionable once again both as a place to live and as a center of the New York gallery world.

Pier 62, abutting the northern end of the Chelsea Piers complex, features tranquil landscaping by Lynden Miller as well as a carousel and an elaborate and popular skate park. Pier 62 merges seamlessly into **Pier 63**, which offers the Lawn Bowl, one of the largest open spaces in Hudson River Park. The transition to Pier 64 is achieved by way of the **Stonefield Native Garden**, set in a secluded glade of weeping willow trees. Designer Meg Webster selected 38 large stones with distinctive personalities from quarries in New York and Pennsylvania. They are arranged to highlight their unique characteristics and to provide a setting for contemplation and quiet recreation.

Unlike its neighbors, **Pier 64** juts out assertively into the Hudson. Past lawns, planted beds, and a grove of oak and crabapple trees, the pier culminates at its western end in an elevated 15-foot knoll that provides expansive views onto the harbor. From here one can look across to leafy **Castle Point** in Hoboken, the site of Stevens Institute of Technology. Slightly to the north is **Weehawken**, best known as the site of the tragic 1804 duel between Alexander Hamilton and Vice President Aaron Burr.

Pier 66 opposite 25th Street has two branches. The southern one is a former Lackawanna Railway float bridge over which freight cars passed onto waiting barges.

One enters along the tracks between an impressive array of timber trusses to reach a vintage caboose. Docked to one side is the John J. Harvey, a retired New York fireboat. Launched in 1931, it had enough power to shoot a jet of water from the river over the roadway of the George Washington Bridge. Harvey returned briefly to service in the wake of the terrorist attacks on September 11, 2001, pumping for 80 hours without stopping until the water mains were restored.

Next to the Harvey, the lightship Frying Pan is open for seasonal tours. Built in 1929, the ship was for over 30 years anchored off Cape Fear, North Carolina. On the other side of the pier a former Lackawanna railway barge has been converted into a popular restaurant, Pier 66 Maritime.

Figure 4.10. Pier 66.

The northern arm of Pier 66 hosts a boathouse for Hudson River Community Sailing. At its western end, revolving with the tides as a reminder of the constant ebb and flow of the Hudson, is a 26-foot waterwheel, *Long Time*, designed by artist Paul Ramirez-Jonas.

The three blocks of Hudson River Park from 26th to 29th Streets are occupied by the Habitat Garden—a fenced ecological area planted with native species and open only for organized visits.

At 22nd Street, West Street curves back westward to become 12th Avenue. It will follow this route northward to 56th Street. The curve creates a triangle of land called **Chelsea Waterside Park**. It was designed by Abel Bainnson Butz and includes a sports field, a fanciful children's playground, and a spacious dog run.

To the east, facing 11th Avenue **The Cortland** at 555 West 22nd Street (2021–2022; RAMSA) is a 25-story condo tower developed, along with a number of other buildings along the river, by Related Companies. Limestone, multicolored and textured brick, and rivet detailing are used to evoke the commercial heritage of the neighborhood. The handsome building is entered through a motor courtyard off 22nd or 23rd Streets. Notice the "holdout" building that eluded the developers on the corner of 22nd Street and 11th Avenue.

The blocks just to the north of the Chelsea Piers complex were for many years the center of Manhattan's warehouse district. By the early

Figure 4.11. *Long Time*, Pier 66.

Figure 4.12. The Cortland.

twentieth century New York was well established both as America's leading port and as a major manufacturing center. By 1900 fully 10 percent of all American manufactured goods were produced in New York and staggering amounts of freight originated in or passed through the city.

From the start, Manhattan's island location, so convenient for docks, presented challenges. Goods arriving by ship for distribution to the rest of the country needed to be transported from the Manhattan piers across the Hudson to the rail lines that terminated on the New Jersey shore. Similarly, freight arriving by train from the south and west needed cross-river transportation to reach the city. To meet these challenges railway companies required large fleets of transport lighters and barges to shuttle railcars across the river as well as extensive yards and terminals on both sides of the Hudson for the transfer of goods from long-distance to local carriers. When the Chelsea

Piers opened in 1910 a large section of the waterfront that once handled freight was ceded to passengers. As a result, cargo traffic was displaced to the north. The new Manhattan cargo terminals clustered in the blocks along the river just south of the High Line's uptown terminus at 30th Street. The New York Central, Hudson River, Erie, B&O, Pennsylvania, and Lehigh Valley Railways all constructed large terminals here. Additional rail yards extended north along the river as far as 72nd Street.

Today a **US Postal Maintenance Facility** at 24th Street and the City's **Department of Sanitation repair shops** occupy the site of the old B&O Railway freight terminal.

In 1931 the Lehigh Valley Railway partnered with the Starrett Corporation to upgrade its terminal facility just to the north. The result is the immense **Starrett-Lehigh Building** that fills the entire square block between 26th and 27th Street east of 12th Avenue.

The Starett-Lehigh Building rose above the railway's old freight yards and was designed so that both trains and trucks could enter the building at ground level. Freight could be transferred directly from trains to vans for delivery, or the goods (and even the trucks themselves!) could be lifted upward on huge elevators to warehouse, display, and manufacturing areas above.

Figure 4.13. Starrett-Lehigh Building.

The building, designed by architects Russell and Walter Cory and Yasuo Matsui, is a modernist classic, made of reinforced concrete with stylish polygonal corners. It is encircled by over eight miles of green steel strip windows separated by concrete and red brick spandrels. It rises 19 floors and encompasses 1.8 million square feet of rentable industrial/warehouse space. Interior supporting columns are set back from the walls to increase light. The soft, rounded contours of the building's eastern and western sections are broken in the center of the block by a taller and sharper-edged brick service core. The entire ensemble is a beautifully integrated symphony of form, line, and color. Today the rail tracks and truck elevators are gone, and the building has been converted into an office and studio complex.

Next door the **New York Terminal Warehouse/Central Stores** (1891; George B. Mallory, Otto M. Beck) is in the process of a radical transformation by COOKFOX Architects into a "destination workplace/engine of enterprise" with work, dining, and retail areas. The handsome brick complex has great presence. Arches are everywhere, creating an impressive composition of solids and voids with many windows retaining their original iron fire shutters. Two rail lines once entered the building through the large central arch on the ground floor, providing a direct connection to the New York Central yards. Inside, the complex, independent sections were customized to serve the needs of specific clients. Some were set aside for the private storage of furniture and household goods, others for theatrical scenery, still others for department store giants like Gimbels and Wanamaker's. Sections with refrigeration were used by grocers, and still others were designated government-bonded warehouses for importers.

Scenic vistas are in short supply in the next blocks. Hudson River Park temporarily disappears to be replaced by the **30th Street Heliport** and park maintenance facilities. Across 12th Avenue lie the 30 tracks of the Long Island Rail Road's **West Side Yard**. Before its construction in 1986, Long Island Rail Road trains coming from the east would deposit their passengers at Penn Station and then return empty to storage yards in Queens. The West Side Yard makes these trips unnecessary. The current rail yard occupies what was once an even larger New York Central freight terminal—the southern terminus of the Hudson River Railroad and the northern end of the High Line.

The West Side Yard is also the site of another major rail connection: the Pennsylvania Railroad's **North River Tunnels**, opened in 1910, pass directly underneath. To this day the twin tubes provide the only direct rail access to New York City from the south. As a part of the creation of the West Side Yard, another tunnel, the **Empire Connection**, was dug to connect Penn Station with the existing Hudson River Railway freight line up the west side of Manhattan. Since 1991 this link has permitted Amtrak trains to access Penn Station from the north. No longer are passengers from Albany and the Hudson Valley forced to change from Grand Central to Penn Station to continue their journey south.

The construction of the West Side Yard was undertaken as part of a much grander redevelopment scheme. At the time of the yard's construction, various proposals were put forward for the use of the air rights overhead. These included a stadium as part of New York's bid for the 2012 Summer Olympics and a new home for Madison Square Garden. In the end, a joint project sponsored by the State of New York, the City, the Metropolitan Transportation Authority, and private developers won out. The result is **Hudson Yards,** a mammoth city within the city built on a platform over the eastern section of the rail yard. In addition to architecturally ambitious apartment and office towers, the complex includes a large shopping mall; the Shed, a performance venue with an enormous rolling roof; and Thomas Heatherwick's ill-conceived and controversial *Vessel*. To many visitors it resembles nothing so much as a gigantic metal waste basket. Future plans call for a second section of Hudson Yards over the western part of the rail yard.

The enormous six-block-long **Jacob K. Javits Convention Center** sits just to the north (1980–1986; James Ingo Freed of Pei Cobb Freed

Figure 4.14. Aerial View of Hudson Yards. *Source:* Alamy.

84 | Along the Hudson

Figure 4.15. Javits Center atrium.

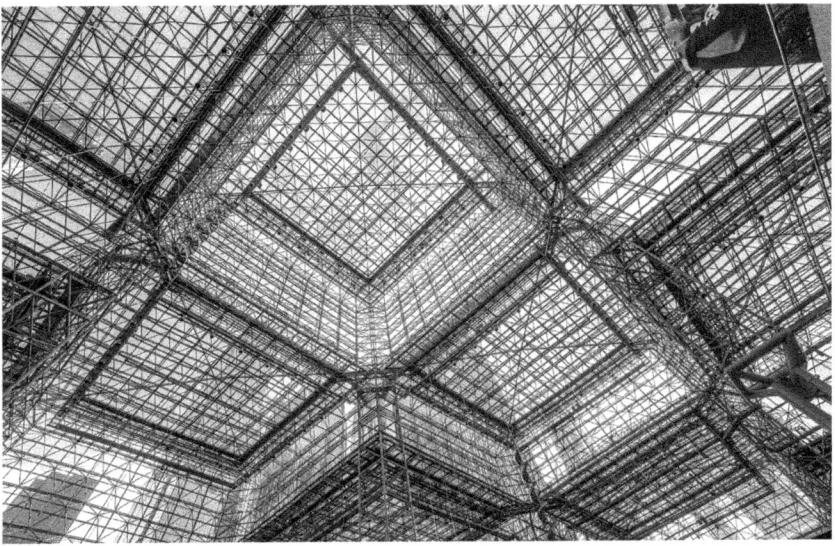

& Partners; later additions and renovations by FXFOWLE, 2010–2013; additional expansion 2016–2021). Built on yet another section of old rail yard, the current building offers 3.3 million square feet of exhibition space. It is a colossus that studiously turns its back on the river. From the west the Javits Center presents a bunker-like wall, pierced by loading entrances off 12th Avenue. And while much of the architectural unity of the original design has been compromised by later additions, the main entry hall running east–west and entered from 11th Avenue is still an impressive space. Freed's stacked glass cubes and supporting spaceframe owe their inspiration to Victorian botanical conservatories and particularly to London's Crystal Palace of 1851. Long isolated, the Javits Center became more accessible in 2015 with the extension of the No. 7 subway line to a new station located midway between the Javits Center and Hudson Yards.

5

The Javits Center to 72nd Street

In the blocks north of the Javits Center, Hudson River Park threads its way through a group of unglamorous service buildings and past Manhattan's last working passenger piers to merge with Riverside Park South and ultimately to enter the Upper West Side.

In the late nineteenth century, the midtown waterfront in the upper 30s was a slaughterhouse district. Animals were grazed in New Jersey and barged across the river or delivered down the Hudson by rail. To facilitate their passage from the piers to the inland abattoirs, mounted cowboys shunted the steers into underground passages beneath 34th and 38th Streets. As late as the 1950s cattle were still being slaughtered here. Clearly, much has changed in the last 70 years.

Pier 76 sits just opposite the Javits Center. The huge facility opened in 1964 as a freight terminal for the United States Lines, replacing three older piers. The United States Lines moved out in 1970, and the once bustling pier began an inglorious stint as a storage pound for towed vehicles. After a significant cleanup, Pier 76 gained new life in 2021 when it was incorporated into the Hudson River Park. With the exception of the arching steel skeleton of the former roof, the main attraction is the 18-foot, 60,000-pound manganese bronze propeller from the retired liner SS *United States*.

Between its launch in 1952 and its retirement in 1969, the ship held the coveted Blue Riband award as the fastest transatlantic passenger liner.

Looking across the river from the end of the pier one can make out the Helix—the spiraling ramp bringing Lincoln Tunnel traffic down from the Union City bluffs to the tunnel entry at river level. The bluffs mark

Figure 5.1. Map 5.

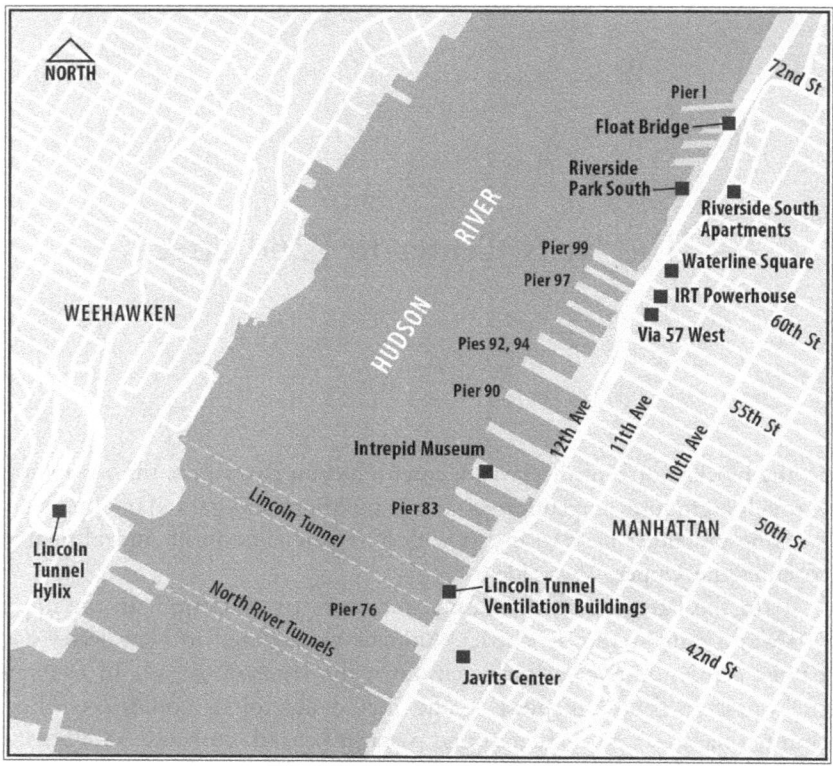

the beginning of the celebrated **Palisades**, the dramatic cliffs that rise to a height of 540 feet above the western bank of the Hudson from this point northward for nearly 20 miles to the Tappan Zee, where the river widens. The Palisades were formed over 200 million years ago, long before the arrival of the glaciers, by an upward flow of magma. They have been regarded as a striking and distinctive feature of the Hudson shoreline since 1524, when explorer Giovanni da Verrazzano likened their unique appearance to "a fence of stakes." The Palisades come into their full natural glory north of the George Washington Bridge; but for the next 140 blocks they form a handsome backdrop for a series of river-level communities on the New Jersey shore, nearly all built on landfill.

Figure 5.2. Pier 76.

Although technically a part of Hudson River Park, **Piers 78** and **79** function as Midtown Manhattan's main ferry terminal. Boats depart from here to Paulus Hook, Hoboken, Weehawken, and Edgewater across the river. The stainless steel sculpture, *Senes* (1973), in the plaza adjacent to the terminal is the work of artist William Crovellow. The ferry terminal building itself wraps around the twin ventilation towers for the **Lincoln Tunnel**, the second of the three vehicular connections between New Jersey and Manhattan.

The Holland Tunnel, downtown at Canal Street, had opened to traffic in 1927, a technical marvel that at a stroke transformed passenger and freight access to Manhattan. So popular was the tunnel that planning for a second crossing between Weehawken and Midtown began almost at once. Construction was underway by 1934, and the first of the Lincoln Tunnel's two-lane tubes opened in December 1937, with additional tubes following in 1945 and 1957. Like its counterparts at the Holland Tunnel, the Lincoln Tunnel's sleek, stylish ventilation buildings were designed by Norwegian architect Erling Owre.

Just to the north, **Pier 81** is now a base for floating restaurants and tour boats. Next door Pier 83 serves the **Circle Line**. Since 1955 it has offered boat tours that circumnavigate Manhattan Island in a little under three hours, offering yet another engaging way to experience the Hudson and its shoreline.

Just opposite Pier 83 lies 42nd Street, one of Manhattan's major crosstown thoroughfares. Times Square is five blocks to the east. In between is the **Hell's Kitchen** neighborhood, originally named by social reformer Jacob Riis and rebranded **Clinton** in recent years to mark its transition from a rough industrial and tenement neighborhood into one of tall apartment towers. Clinton is popular with young professionals, particularly those working in the theater industry. The New York consulate of the People's Republic of China occupies a portion of the modern apartment building at the northeast corner of 42nd Street and 12th Avenue. To the north the New York Headquarters of **UPS** fills the entire block between 43rd and 44th Streets. It's building is appropriately decked out in the company's trademark shades of brown.

Extending 1,000 feet, **Pier 84** is among the longest in Hudson River Park. Notable today for its boathouse and interactive fountain, the pier was erected in 1924 to serve the Cunard Line. Passenger service here ended in 1975, and the pier subsequently served as a parking lot and as a

Figure 5.3. Pier 83.

concert venue for performances by such artists as Los Lobos, B. B. King, Iggy Pop, and Jimmy Buffett. After a comprehensive restoration, Pier 84 became a part of Hudson River Park in 2006. The hook-shaped extension at the western end of the pier was once used to guide transatlantic liners to their berths. Note how, just as we saw in Chelsea, 12th Avenue veers slightly to the east here to accommodate the rewatering necessary for the construction of longer piers.

Pier 86 is the home of the ***Intrepid* Sea, Air & Space Museum**, one of the only places on the Hudson today where a large vessel is actually moored. The museum was founded in 1982 as a home for the retired aircraft carrier USS *Intrepid*, built in 1943. In subsequent years the museum was expanded and now includes the *Enterprise* space shuttle, a Concorde supersonic passenger plane, 28 additional aircraft, and the submarine USS *Growler*. A bridge over 12th Avenue facilitates pedestrian access.

Completed in 1935, the **New York Passenger Ship Terminal** (originally Piers 88, 90, 92, and 94) was constructed to accommodate transatlantic liners which had outgrown the capacity of the Chelsea Piers downtown.

Figure 5.4. Passenger Ship Terminal in 1950s. *Source:* Alamy.

Faced with the continuing decline of transatlantic passenger service during the 1960s, the city sold Piers 92 and 94 and renovated Piers 88 and 90 into the **Manhattan Cruise Ship Terminal**. Today the few remaining transatlantic liners dock at a terminal in Red Hook, Brooklyn.

Pier 88's most famous/infamous moment took place in February of 1942. The flagship of the French Line, SS *Normandie*, then the world's largest and most glamorous liner, was docked at the pier. In the aftermath of Pearl Harbor, the ship had been seized by the US government and was in the process of being converted into a troop carrier. A fire broke out on board, and efforts to contain it failed. The ship rolled over and sank—a total loss.

Happily, some of the *Normandie*'s extraordinary Art Deco fittings have survived in museums and on the facade of the church of Our Lady of Lebanon in Brooklyn Heights.

The remaining parts of the 1935 Passenger Ship Terminal, **Piers 92** and **94**, have been converted into a venue for trade shows and special events. With over 200,000 square feet of available exhibition space, the piers are second in size only to the Javits Center. The poor condition of Pier 92 has in recent years, however, prevented its active use.

It is worth pausing to take a quick look at the design of the Hustler Club on the corner of 52nd Street, just across 12th Avenue from

Figure 5.5. SS *Normandie* sinking at Pier 88. *Source:* Alamy.

the passenger piers. It is an extraordinary confection of classical pilasters, capitals, pediments, reliefs, and even a small temple all stuck willy-nilly to the outside of a warehouse. **DeWitt Clinton Park** just to the north offers a more salubrious environment. It is named in honor of the New York governor and New York City mayor who championed the transformational construction of the Erie Canal.

Hudson River Park emerges again just north of Pier 94 at **Clinton Cove**, an open green space connecting Piers 95, 96, and 97. In addition to green lawns and renewed access to the water, the main feature of the Cove is *Private Passage* (2005), a sculpture by Malcom Cochran. Inside the 30-foot-long wine bottle is a fanciful interpretation of a stateroom on the Cunard liner *Queen Mary*.

Clinton Cove brings us near the northern end of the formidable Hudson River Bulkhead. The six-foot granite blocks that mark the upper layer of a complex supporting system beneath the river can be seen at several locations in Hudson River Park, including this one. You can get a good view from the deck on the small **Pier 95**.

Pier 96 nearby is home to the Manhattan Community Boathouse, offering free kayaking lessons from its river-level launching deck. Next door, **Pier 97** was built between 1921 and 1934 for the Swedish American Line. It was here, in 1956, that the liner MS *Stockholm* tied up after its fatal collision with the Italian liner *Andrea Doria*. Used in subsequent years by the city's Department of Sanitation and later as a concert venue, Pier 97 has been redesigned with recreational spaces and elevated lounge areas.

Via 57 West, 625 West 57th Street (2016; Bjarke Ingles Group) is hard to miss—a dramatic 35-story stainless steel wedge or hyperbolic paraboloid that swoops upward to a peak at the northeast.

The architects describe the building as a "man-made mountainside" where wall and roof merge to become one. An enormous cutout in the center of the building creates an elevated private interior courtyard that allows sunlight to enter the heart of the huge structure. The design is a conscious effort to combine the features of a traditional courtyard apartment building with those of a skyscraper. The latter aspect of the project is most notable on the vertiginous north facade—a metal curtain wall animated by window projections arranged in a fishbone pattern.

Via 57 West marks a point of transition on the riverfront. Just to the west are the northern terminus of Hudson River Park and the last of the huge commercial piers that once lined the Hudson all the way up from the Battery. This is the spot where Manhattan's former working waterfront gives

Figure 5.6. Via 57 West.

way to a nearly unbroken series of parks and residential neighborhoods; industrial and service structures are replaced by greenery and apartment towers. In a similar fashion, the sloping skyscraper facade of Via 57 West echoes the changing character of the highway that separates inland neighborhoods from the river. Here 12th Avenue, which has run as a surface highway for five miles, now rises to first become the elevated Joe DiMaggio Highway and ultimately the Henry Hudson Parkway. The natural terrain changes here too. From the Battery to this point, Manhattan Island has been comparatively level. From this point north, the Hudson shore is dominated by a series of hills, separated by narrow valleys. These heights provide often stunning views over the river to the New Jersey shore.

One final reminder of the neighborhood's industrial past remains: the **IRT Powerhouse** (1902–1904; Stanford White of McKim, Mead & White; later additions and changes).

Figure 5.7. IRT Powerhouse, 1904. Wikimedia Commons. Public domain.

The debut of the IRT subway in 1904 forever changed New York, opening new neighborhoods for development and dramatically altering long-standing patterns of where people lived and worked. Electric power was the subway's lifeblood, and the sprawling system required a powerhouse that was, at the time of its completion, the world's largest. The IRT generated its power here until the line was taken over by the city in 1940. In 1959 the old generators were removed, and Con Edison converted the building to a steam plant. Today, steam generated here is fed into a 105-mile network of pipes to heat and cool nearly 1,500 buildings in Manhattan south of 96th Street.

The original powerhouse was an engineering marvel; two buildings (a boiler house and a generating room) were handsomely wrapped in an architecturally unified envelope. Coal was delivered to the riverbank by boat and then carried via an underground conveyor beneath 12th Avenue before being hoisted to bunkers at the top of the building. Ash was removed back across 12th Avenue by a parallel route.

The IRT was determined that the new powerhouse would be "an architectural landmark," aligned with the prevailing principles of the City

Beautiful Movement. Instead of employing Heins & LaFarge, who designed the IRT's stations, they chose the prestigious firm of McKim, Mead & White and allocated additional funds to ensure that the building was suitably embellished. Stanford White did not let them down, creating a dignified classical design in granite and Roman brick that contemporary critics described as a worthy home for a museum or library. White enriched his facade with splendid terracotta details. Note in particular the spirited eagles that crown each window arch and the distinctive cartouches in the capital of each pilaster. Each features a pinecone surrounded by wings and lightning bolts.

Unfortunately, the building has suffered over the years. The handsome original cornice is gone, along with the majestic row of six smokestacks that once echoed the funnels of the transatlantic liners docked nearby. The original Roman windows have been much modified, and a bland, characterless addition was grafted onto the west side of the building in 1951. Still, many of the handsome original details survive as a testament to a moment when important civic buildings, even utilitarian ones, deserved serious dignified architectural treatment.

Pier 98 was originally built to service the powerhouse and continues today as a Con Edison fuel transfer station. Next door, **Pier 99**, the last of the Hudson's numbered piers, is used by the city's sanitation department as a marine transfer station for recyclables. The current pier buildings, with their suggestion of a temple pediment, are the work of Richard Dattner, who was responsible for the architectural design of the stretch of Hudson River Park from 29th Street to this pier. In 1990 artist Stephen Antonakos designed the colorful neon installation that brings nighttime life to the pier facade.

In the early twentieth century, large numbers of African Americans relocated from Greenwich Village to the westside blocks north of 59th Street. The new neighborhood became known as San Juan Hill, reputedly in honor of the Black veterans of the Spanish American War who settled here. Until the rise of Harlem in the 1920s, San Juan Hill was the center for Black life in New York City. In later years, before urban renewal efforts led to the neighborhood's destruction—to allow for the erection of public housing and of Lincoln Center—the neighborhood attracted a large Puerto Rican community.

For much of the twentieth century, the land from West End Avenue to the river between 59th and 72nd Streets was occupied by the New York Central's enormous **60th Street Rail Yard**, a vast and gritty complex of sidings, warehouses, piers, and float bridges. There was even a locomotive roundhouse. At its peak, the 60th Street yard handled a remarkable variety of

Figure 5.8. The 60th Street Rail Yard, 1924. *Source:* Alamy.

goods from dairy products to automobiles and construction supplies shipped to New York on nearly all of the country's great railways. The bankruptcy of the New York Central and then of its successor railways (PennCentral, ConRail), along with a dramatic decline in rail freight traffic, led in the mid-1970s to the closing of the yard. The removal of the tracks freed up one of the last major undeveloped parcels of land along the Hudson. The opportunity was in many ways similar to that offered by the creation of the landfill now occupied by Battery Park City, and a large number of competing projects were quickly floated.

In 1985 Donald Trump gained control of the former yards and proclaimed his intention to erect the tallest building in the world, along with additional structures containing 7,600 apartments. The plan also included the creation of a new park along the river and the burying of both the remaining railway tracks and the parallel sections of the highway. Financing challenges soon appeared, and a long series of alternative development plans were proposed and rejected. Trump took on partners and ultimately sold his controlling interest. Finally, in 1997 construction began on the creation of a new apartment neighborhood on elevated land overlooking what was to become a southward extension of Riverside Park. The elevated DiMaggio Highway was rebuilt along its original path, and the railway tracks were routed through a tunnel behind the apartment buildings.

In the course of planning the redevelopment of the rail yard, a parcel of land between 59th and 61st Streets became separated from the larger section to the north. This ultimately became the architecturally ambitious **Waterline Square**, three glassy, angular buildings arranged around a central park with boardwalks and water features. At the southwest corner the 37-story **One Waterline Square** (2015–2019; Richard Meier & Partners) is a busy composition that is something of a departure from Meier's usual cool, gridded mode. Next door, the pared towers of **Two Waterline Square** (2019; Kohn Pedersen Fox) offer more sleek glass, along with dramatic cantilevers and aggressive angles. **Three Waterline Square** (2019; Rafael Vinoly) to the east is an irregular faceted crystalline structure with several provocative cutout balconies. Together and separately the buildings are a dramatic if somewhat awkward crowd. In addition to elaborate amenities, all three buildings include both rental and condo units.

Figure 5.9. Waterline Square.

The remaining Riverside South apartment buildings unfold northward along a new street, Riverside Boulevard, in a bland attempt to combine the graceful sweep of the original Riverside Drive with the drama of the paired Art Deco towers of Central Park West. The eleven river-facing buildings, completed between 1998 and 2008 to designs by Philip Johnson/Allan Richie Architects and Costas Kondylis, are a formulaic stretch of skyline offering little aside from great views of the river for residents.

Close by, the noisy elevated **Joe DiMaggio Highway** runs parallel to the full length of Riverside Boulevard. From 1929 to 1973 the original West Side Highway ran all the way north to 72nd Street on an elevated trestle. After the Westway Project was abandoned in 1985, the old highway was, as we have seen, gradually reconstructed as an urban boulevard running at ground level as far as 59th Street. The remaining section of the elevated highway north of 59th Street was retained, widened, straightened, reinforced, and renamed for the celebrated Yankees center fielder. It now connects the street-level portions of the highway to the south with the Henry Hudson Parkway at 72nd Street. (Long-term plans call for a revival of the abandoned attempt to rebuild the highway in what would be a new tunnel under Riverside Boulevard.)

Figure 5.10. Riverside South.

While Donald Trump originally acquired a development option on the entire rail yard site, in 1992 after repeated unsuccessful efforts to secure approval for his plans and multiple financial setbacks, he agreed to relinquish control of the river-level land to allow for the creation of a 24-acre park. Today **Riverside Park South**, nestled under the protective shadow of the DiMaggio Highway, links Hudson River Park with the original Riverside Park to the north. Construction began in 2001 to designs by Thomas Balsley with final work, still underway, financed by a levy on the apartment buildings along Riverside Boulevard. Balsley's design combines a riprap shoreline with landscaping, intertwining paths, and boardwalks. Plantings are understated: lawns, groves of trees, and clumps of marsh grasses. Pavilions and seating areas, including a Solstice Bench at 63rd Street, punctuate the shoreline.

The most distinctive feature of the park, however, is Balsley's enthusiastic embrace of the area's railway heritage. Among the key features of the old rail yard were a series of six piers (identified by letters to distinguish them from the numbered piers to the south) and three **float bridges**. The latter

Figure 5.11. The 69th Street float bridge.

allowed railcars to be transferred to barges (floats) for transportation across the Hudson to and from yards in Weehawken. In the early years of the twentieth century between 3,000 and 5,000 freight cars made this journey every day. The float bridges that made this possible were complex works of engineering that allowed eight cars to be loaded onto a float in ten minutes while the bridges simultaneously adjusted to the effects of wind and the river current. Today the picturesque remains of the float bridge at 69th Street, listed on the Historic American Engineering Record, is the lone survivor.

Except for the 69th Street float bridge, all that remains of the original piers are lines of piles in the river. In contrast to the piers farther south, which extended at right angles to the riverbank, the piers and float bridges here were angled into the river at 55 degrees to facilitate loading. Today, similarly angled walkways branch off the main park paths to meet the river where several of the piers once stood. At other locations, old stone foundations and bulkheads have been preserved in small coves. The cement walkway surrounding the cove at 62nd Street has been incised with the names of places and firms that once shipped goods to this site. Nearby, between 61st and 62nd Streets, **New York Central switching locomotive 8625** occupies a place of honor. And in yet one more poignant railroad reference, benches in the two seating areas near 66th Street bear the names of the now vanished lines that once delivered freight to the yards here.

At the far northern end of the park near 72nd Street, a baseball field has been carefully and deliberately shaped to recall the locomotive roundhouse that once stood nearby. To the west, **Pier I** has been reconstructed, extending 715 feet out into the river at its original angle from a pleasant café on shore. The pier, with its distinctive undulating profile, offers fine views.

Figure 5.12. Seating in Riverside Park South.

Figure 5.13. Highway overpass, Riverside Park South.

To the east, the space under the elevated highway provides a route for a popular bicycle and jogging path, a component of the Hudson River Greenway. Work continues nearby on ball fields and recreational areas. At the center of the park at 66th Street a series of terraces and steps lead down from a plaza at Riverside Boulevard, past planted beds and a fountain, to pass under the highway to the river level.

But where did the railway go? Currently the tracks north from Penn Station, those carrying Amtrak's Empire Service, run underground in a tunnel. South of 60th Street that tunnel passes just to the west of 10th Avenue. At 60th Street it slants farther westward to run behind the apartment buildings on Riverside Boulevard to 72nd Street, where the tunnel angles again to continue under Riverside Park to 124th Street. There the tracks emerge from the ground to continue north along the bank of the river.

A glimpse of the railway can be had just south of 72nd Street beneath a wildly complex mix of old and new viaducts. Here the DiMaggio Highway passes over a remnant of the old Miller Highway to link with a new connection between Riverside Boulevard and West 72nd Street. The railway is hidden beneath, adjacent to an unexpected skatepark and basketball court.

6

72nd Street to 110th Street

As we have seen, Manhattan's systematically developed commercial waterfront ended with Pier 99 at 59th Street. A series of mammoth rail yards, subsequently redeveloped, filled the following blocks. At 72nd Street those rail yards gave way to a haphazard series of small wharfs, construction yards, and squatter encampments all scattered along the tracks at the base of a steep slope leading up to highlands above the river. By the middle of the nineteenth century this stretch of shoreline was ripe for development and the stage was set for the creation of both **Riverside Park** and **Riverside Drive**, one of Manhattan's great residential neighborhoods.

Planning for the park and drive began around 1865 when William R. Martin, president of the West Side Association and an advocate for the development of the still largely vacant land between the Hudson and Central Park, proposed the creation of a new park along the river. The idea was taken up by Andrew Haswell Green and the Central Park Commissioners, who were legally responsible for planning the layout of the entire west side of Manhattan north of 59th Street. Together they secured state funds to purchase land, and in 1875 Frederick Law Olmsted was hired to lay out Riverside Park and an adjacent vehicular drive.

Riverside Drive (originally Riverside Avenue) opened to traffic in 1880, although it was not until 1902, with the completion of a viaduct over 96th Street, that an uninterrupted roadway stretched from 72nd to 125th Street. Riverside Drive was from the start a gracefully curving and undulating boulevard. It accommodated the natural terrain and offered frequent stopping places from which to admire the vista over the river. The hope was that

Figure 5.1. Map 5.

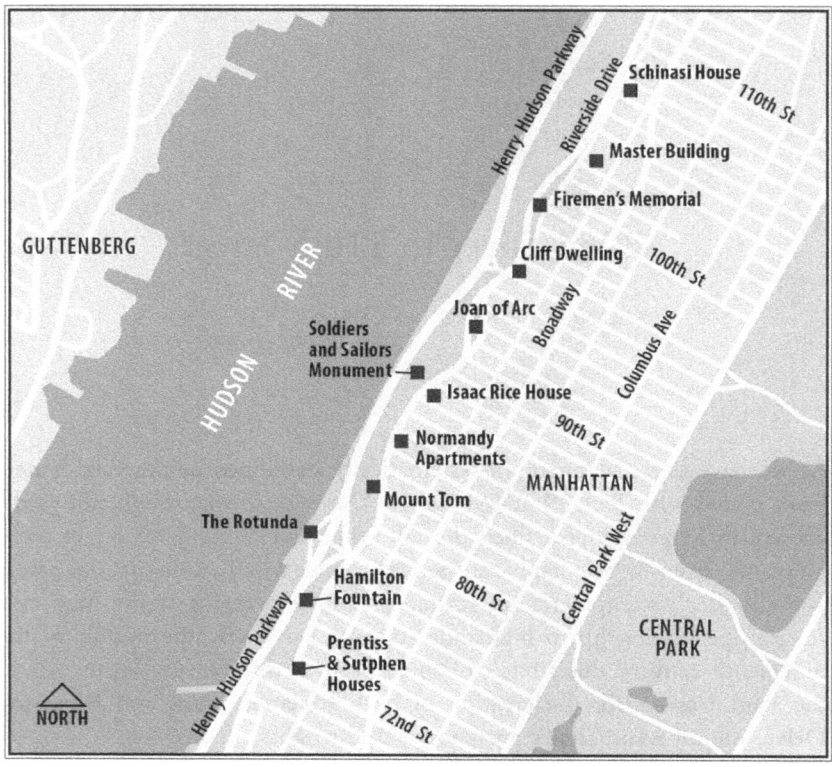

the elegant new street would not only spur residential development on the Upper West Side (then called the West End) but also emerge as a rival to Fifth Avenue as a preferred address for New York's wealthy. This did not immediately come to pass. Development lagged along the new drive, retarded by the area's remote location, a lack of nearby public transportation, and a fear of biting winter winds from the river. It took a while, but Riverside Drive did eventually attract a number of impressive mansions and villas, some substantial rowhouses, and in the end some of Manhattan's most desirable apartment buildings.

Olmsted's initial concept for the park to the west of Riverside Avenue may also have played a role in hindering development. The celebrated designer made no attempt to widen or develop the steep and narrow slope leading down to the rubbish heaps, shanties, wharfs, and construction yards along the shore. The effect of these nearby eyesores was compounded by the presence of the railway, which by the turn of the century had expanded to six tracks. Discussions about the possibility of roofing over those tracks began as early as 1913, but the exhaust from the steam locomotives then in use made this impracticable. It was not until 1923 when the state passed the so-called Kaufman Act mandating electric traction for all trains running within the city that planning for a tunnel began in earnest. Various schemes were put forward, but until 1934, in the midst of the Great Depression, little was accomplished. In that year Robert Moses became the city's Parks Commissioner. With funds from the WPA and over 6,000 laborers, Moses set to work on a dramatic reconstruction of the Manhattan waterfront north of 72nd Street, including an extension of the West Side Highway northward to the Bronx. As part of the mammoth scheme, the rail line was relocated to run in a tunnel from 72nd to 124th Street, and Riverside Park was dramatically expanded and reconstructed.

Today Riverside Park remains much as Moses left it when his project was completed in 1937. Beyond the western parapet and walkway along Riverside Drive, the park drops off steeply down steps and ramps to meandering paths through woods and planted areas. At the bottom of the slope is a broad promenade covering the concrete tunnel through which run the

Figure 6.2. Riverside Park looking south from 120th Street. *Source:* Alamy.

tracks of the former New York Central Railway—today's Amtrak Empire Service. Still farther down, beyond the promenade are the six lanes of the Henry Hudson Parkway along with 132 acres of landfill, added by Moses to accommodate playgrounds, ball fields, tennis courts, and sections of the new parkway. A narrow strip along the shore itself provides a riverside route for the Hudson River Greenway. Moses's achievement is a planning and design triumph, even if in the process of removing one pedestrian barrier to the river (the railway) he added another (the highway).

Because Riverside Drive and Riverside Park were conceived from the start as a unit, and because the park itself is so narrow, the best way to explore both is to walk along Riverside Drive, beginning at 72nd Street.

The **Chatsworth Apartments**, 344 West 72nd Street (1902–1904; John Scharsmith) is an impressive Beaux Arts design that provides an attractive anchor to the southern end of Riverside Park. The building in brick and stone displays exuberantly applied detailing and a prominent mansard roof crowning a facade enriched with projecting window bays. The Chatsworth was conceived as a high-end building with large apartments and a rooftop conservatory, as well as such amenities as an in-house café, a barbershop, and a beauty salon. The building was a success, and a small, linked addition was added to the east in 1905.

In 1899 Lydia Prentiss and Mary Tier Sutphen each acquired building lots on 72nd Street at the foot of Riverside Drive. By this time these were already covered by covenants that limited construction to single-family stone residences. In a conscious effort to set an example that would "induce wealthy and select families . . . to live there," Sutphen and Prentiss agreed to develop their properties in close coordination according to designs by the fashionable townhouse architect C. P. H. Gilbert.

The **Lydia Prentiss Residence** (now the Islamic Culture Center of New York) at 1 Riverside Drive (1899–1901; C. P. H. Gilbert) is a solid five-story limestone composition with an American basement, prominent curved corner bay topped by a turret, and a full mansard roof with copper cladding. The curve of the street and the unusual width of the building lot ensure that the Prentiss House receives good natural light from two sides. The design also creates a close visual connection to the adjacent and complementary **Mary Tier Sutphen House**, completed by Gilbert in 1902. It stands across a wedge-shaped courtyard at 311 West 72nd Street. The two houses form a unified ensemble that turns the corner to Riverside Drive with great style. Alas, the standard set by the Prentiss and Sutphen houses

Figure 6.3. Prentiss and Sutphen Houses.

did not hold. The lot at **2 Riverside Drive** remained undeveloped until 1964 when the present dreary apartment house was erected.

High style returns dramatically at 3 Riverside Drive with the **Philip and Maria Kleeberg House** (1896–1898; C. P. H. Gilbert). The Kleeberg residence shows Gilbert working in his preferred French Renaissance mode. The main facade features a richly ornamented, putti-enriched portal and a three-story projecting bay strikingly detailed with pilasters, foliate carvings, and shields. The composition is crowned by an impressive set of pinnacled gables and a fine tile roof. There is a charming south-facing balcony, also richly embellished, at the fourth level. Long divided into apartments, the house is currently being reconverted into an elaborate single-family dwelling. The remainder of the block is filled by **5 Riverside Drive**, a handsome Art Deco tower completed in 1936 to designs by Russell Boak & Hyman Paris. It was among the first of the new apartment houses to be built on Riverside Drive following Robert Moses's renovation of Riverside Park.

Just across the street in a circular plaza is Penelope Jencks's sculpted memorial to **Eleanor Roosevelt**, unveiled in 1996. The figure of the first lady stands amidst trees and plantings. Quotations from both Roosevelt and Adlai Stevenson are inscribed in the pavement nearby.

The full block between 73rd and 74th Streets was long occupied by the immense 86-room **Charles Schwab House**, designed as a French chateau in 1905 by architect Maurice Hebert for the president of the Carnegie Steel Company. Always a maverick, Schwab chose to live not on Fifth Avenue near his partners Carnegie and Frick, but on the then-remote Riverside Drive. From the start the house was something of a white elephant, and Schwab at one point pressed the city to acquire it as a residence for the mayor. Fiorello La Guardia declined. In the end, the house only survived until 1948, when it was replaced by the present apartment block.

Houses by C. P. H. Gilbert once filled the full length of the block from 74th to 75th Streets. The southernmost building of the group, the home of George H. Macy, was demolished to make way for the current **22 Riverside** (1930–1931; William Paris of Boak & Paris). This fine Art Deco tower features cutout corner windows and an interesting composition of terraces and penthouses up top. Next door, **numbers 23 and 24** are twins, built together between 1895 and 1897 by Gilbert in a simplified version of his preferred François Premier style. The final house on the block, **25 Riverside Drive** (322 West 75th Street), with its impressive corner pavilion and echoing bay to the

Figure 6.4. 25 Riverside Drive.

south, was designed by Gilbert in the same years for publisher Henry Vail. Here the architect drew his inspiration from Italian Renaissance models. Note the fine Roman brick and carefully executed stone detailing. Gilbert also designed the three handsome townhouses immediately to the east on 75th Street.

33 Riverside Drive (1927; George F. Pelham) is an architecturally unremarkable sixteen-story brick block perhaps best known as having been the home of both George and Ira Gershwin. The brothers rented adjoining penthouses in the building in 1929, moving from their former home on 103rd Street. (The prior owner of the lot at 33 Riverside was Sergei Rachmaninoff, who sold his house there to allow construction of the current building.)

The pair of solid Romanesque townhouses at **35 and 36 Riverside** date to 1889 and were originally part of group of four designed by the firm of Lamb & Rich. The remaining buildings are filled with personality. The tile roof is pierced with distinctive pointed dormers on number 36, and there is a hidden servants' entry tucked under the steps of number 35.

At the time of his death in 1890, businessman and politician Robert Hamilton, great grandson of Alexander, bequeathed $9,000 to the city for the erection of an ornamental fountain on Riverside Drive. Warren & Wetmore provided the design and pulled out all the stops. The **Robert Ray Hamilton Fountain** (west side of Riverside Drive at 76th Street) in warm Tennessee

Figure 6.5. Robert Ray Hamilton Fountain.

marble features a spread-winged eagle, a coat of arms with a rampant horse, a dolphin head spout, and two basins, the lower one convenient for the use of passing horses. The fountain was installed in 1903. After a long period in disrepair, it was restored in 2009 by the Riverside Park Conservancy.

The picturesque block of **Riverside Drive between 76th and 77th Streets** is almost unique in retaining its original appearance. Erected between 1896 and 1898, all except the house at 42 Riverside Drive are the work of Clarence True—an extraordinary architect and developer whose buildings dot the Upper West Side. During his career he erected an estimated 250 houses.

Clarence True thought big. By 1896 he had purchased virtually every available lot along Riverside Drive south of 84th Street and designed a plan for the development of those eight blocks into what Christopher Gray called "a panorama of picturesque rooflines and oak-paneled interiors." Unlike most designers, who were happy to work to a formula for such large projects, True juggled the widths, depths, and floor plans of his houses to ensure variety and gain living space. Some houses have square layouts rather than a more typical narrow rectangular plans. A number of his corner houses, such as 46 Riverside Drive at the corner of 77th Street, although they appear from the outside to contain several separate dwellings, are in fact a single residence. If True experimented with his floor plans, he was more consistent with the style of his elevations. The architect, who began his career in the studio of Richard Upjohn, most often drew inspiration from Dutch or Elizabethan prototypes. He loved stepped gables, bold dormers, prominent quoins, and corner towers.

True developed the present block in two sections: a group of three houses on Riverside and 76th Street followed by a second group of six along Riverside Drive and down the south side of 77th Street. Somehow the building lot between these two groups escaped him. 42 Riverside was erected between 1897 and 1899 to designs by Charles Buek.

His design is modestly more French in character, but it is not jarringly out of place. Buek is probably best known as the architect of Astor Row, a singular model housing development commissioned by the eponymous family on West 130th Street.

In the next block **52 Riverside Drive** (1926; Deutsch & Schneider) is notable for its exuberant terracotta. Nearby **67 Riverside Drive** (1906–1907; George F. Pelham) at the southeast corner of 79th Street features some vigorous detailing: bold stone brackets, swags, shell ornament, and iron-railed balconies.

Figure 6.6. Riverside Drive, 76th to 77th Streets.

Across Riverside Drive, 79th Street descends to the central architectural feature of Riverside Park—**the Rotunda.**

This inventive and complex structure provides automobile access to and from the Henry Hudson Parkway by way of an upper-level traffic circle. At the center of the circle an open courtyard with a fountain admits light and air to a sloping arcade descending to the waterfront. The passages behind the arcade, beautifully roofed with Guastavino tiles, accommodate a popular seasonal café that spreads onto a terrace overlooking a marina. Ramps to the north and south lead to a parking garage on the lowest level. In addition to all of this, the complex also accommodates the railway. It runs in a tunnel just to the east of the parkway.

The entire composition in stone-faced concrete is the work of architect Clinton Lloyd and landscape designer Gilmore Clarke, working under the guidance of the ubiquitous Robert Moses. Together they have created a remarkable complex of interlocking geometries that masterfully serves the

Figure 6.7. The Rotunda, Riverside Park. Courtesy of Municipal Archives, City of New York. Used with permission.

needs of multiple constituencies. The rotunda is currently in the middle of a major restoration. The nearby marina is simultaneously being redesigned, displacing boat owners, some of whom had made the marina their home for decades.

Back on Riverside Drive, the blocks ahead contain additional examples of Charles True's work. The Riverside Drive/West 80th–81st Street Historic District is home to no less than 21 extant houses by the architect and developer, all built on speculation. The varied and picturesque group from **74** to **77 Riverside Drive** dates to 1898–1899 and shows True working in his favored Jacobean mode, including one of the architect's favorite motifs: a corner tower at the intersection of Riverside and 80th Street. To the north, past the apartment hotel at 80 Riverside (1926–1927; Maurice Deutsch), there is another block of True's work, culminating once again with a corner tower at West 81st Street.

At 81st Street Riverside Drive, stubbornly refusing to conform to the Manhattan street grid, begins a series of graceful curves leading past a row of large apartment houses. Most of these date to the 1920s and 1930s and were designed by such specialist firms as George F. Pelham, Schwartz & Gross, and Boak & Paris.

One last group of houses by Clarence True remains at **103–109 Riverside Drive**. The final house in the row on the corner of 83rd Street is notable both for its impressive entry portal and for its bold, crenellated tower, curiously flattened on its western side. This profile is the result of a neighbor's lawsuit against the home's first owner alleging that the original round tower extended beyond the official property line. It took a decade, but the complainant won, and in 1911 the offending curve was removed along with projecting bays on the adjacent houses to create a flat, uniform street line.

Figure 6.8. 103–109 Riverside Drive.

Across the way, just inside Riverside Park is a rocky outcropping dubbed **Mount Tom**. Tradition has it that the name was coined by Edgar Allan Poe, who in 1844 lived nearby on 84th Street in a farmhouse owned by the Brennan family. Poe allegedly received the inspiration for "The Raven" while seated on this outcropping and named the spot for his landlord's youngest son.

The massive twin buildings of **110–118 Riverside** (1928–1929; Gronenberg & Leuchtag) occupy the full block between 83rd and 84th Streets. **125 Riverside Drive** (1904–1907; Samuel B. Ogden), a rental building in the next block, has considerably more personality. Twin towers frame an improbably deep light well piercing far into the building. The shorter building to the south is a part of the same complex.

137 Riverside Drive, The Clarendon, at the corner of 86th Street, was built in 1906–1907 to designs by Charles E. Birge. The building is a near twin to its neighbor to the south, **The Dorchester** (1909; Neville & Bagge). Both are unprepossessing compositions, except perhaps for the assertive brick and limestone striping on the tenth floor. The Clarendon, however, is notable as the longtime home of publisher William Randolph Hearst, who moved there in 1908, converting the top three floors into a single 30-room apartment. When the Clarendon's owners refused his request to add a 100-foot-long vaulted tapestry gallery on the roof, Hearst promptly bought the entire building. In time the publisher and his art collection moved on to the West Coast, the building was sold, and his huge apartment subdivided. The copper mansard housing the gallery and the rooftop cupola he added are still visible on the Riverside Drive front of the building.

One of the last great apartment buildings erected in New York before World War II, the block-filling, twin-towered **Normandy Apartments** at 140 Riverside Drive (1938–1939; Emery Roth & Sons) is a major landmark. The symmetrical, H-plan building is entered through a central recessed garden court. Twenty-story wings rise to either side. In its plan and elevation, the Normandy is very much the peer of such other classic buildings by Roth as the San Remo and Beresford on Central Park West. In terms of style, the building is something of a hybrid. The Normandy rises from a limestone base with streamlined horizontal striations; the corners are curved, and the casement windows set in the warm light brick walls are without trim. Zippy mosaic decorations adorn the main entry. For all of this modernity, historical elements occasionally slip in. Renaissance urns and balustrades turn up in the garden courts; and there are simplified classical pilasters, cornices, and aediculae on the towers. The blend, if slightly schizophrenic, is a pleasing one; and the building is a distinguished presence that dominates this section of Riverside Drive.

Figure 6.9. Normandy apartments.

The **Isaac L. Rice House** "Villa Julia" (1901–1903; Herts & Tallant; alterations 1908, C. P. H. Gilbert) on the corner of 89th Street is one of only two surviving freestanding mansions on Riverside Drive. The house is the work of two of New York's leading theatrical architects, who are probably best known for the Lyceum and New Amsterdam Theaters. This background likely accounts for the dramatic siting of the Rice House and for its eye-catching but difficult to describe architectural style. The building is essentially an Italian villa, symmetrical and carefully composed on all sides. Dark red brick, laid in Flemish bond, is accented with bold marble detailing to create a striking composition. On its west side, the house is set well back from the street, perched high at the top of a terraced garden. One enters at the second-floor level through an imposing recessed marble portal set within a tall arch. That arch forms the central component of a larger composition that includes a cornice and flanking windows supported by Tuscan columns. Altogether they create what is essentially an expanded serliana that stretches across the entire facade. On 89th Street a two-story curving bay shelters a porte-cochere under heavy segmental arches, which

Figure 6.10. Isaac L. Rice House.

provides access to the ground floor. The sculpture under the pediment between the two arches depicts six children, perhaps members of the Rice family, holding emblems of the liberal arts. Up top, a dramatic projecting cornice and carefully placed chimneys complete the distinctive composition.

Rice and his wife were an interesting couple. Born in Bavaria, he was an author, a lawyer, an early proponent of electric vehicles, and a well-known chess player. Julia Rice was a physician who pressed successfully for laws limiting street and river noise. In 1907 Rice sold his house to Solomon Schinasi, a tobacco importer. We will encounter his brother Morris's house at 351 Riverside Drive, the only other survivor from the 30 freestanding mansions that once dotted Riverside Drive. Today the landmarked Rice House is the home of the Yeshiva Ketana.

The **Soldiers' and Sailors' Monument** (1897–1902; Charles W. & Arthur A. Stoughton and Paul E. M. Duboy) presides over Riverside Park at 89th Street. The New York legislature authorized the erection of a monument to honor state residents who had fought in the Civil War in 1869, but the project languished until 1893. A site on Grand Army Plaza at Fifth Avenue and 59th Street was initially chosen, and a competition for a memorial there was held in 1897. Opposition from various constituencies, however, prompted a relocation to Riverside Drive and 83rd Street. This location too was ultimately rejected in favor of the current site on a promontory overlooking the river. Additional time was required to revise Stoughton & Stoughton's original design to suit the new site. Paul Duboy, best known for the design of the Ansonia Hotel on Broadway, joined the project to manage the carved ornament, and it was not until 1900 that construction actually began. The unveiling of the 100-foot-tall monument took place on Memorial Day in 1902.

The circular monument is closely based on the ancient Athenian Choragic Monument to Lysicrates, a frequent source of inspiration for architects during the turn-of-the-century City Beautiful Movement. Twelve Corinthian columns rise from a rusticated marble base pierced by a single door. The

Figure 6.11. Soldiers' and Sailors' Monument.

columns support a conical roof topped by a finial. The monument is set on a series of carefully planned and richly paved terraces embellished with benches, canon, and a flagpole. The entire composition is beautifully sited on a curve in Riverside Drive to ensure a dramatic view when approached from the south. The flagpole, on the other hand, is placed to terminate the westward vista down 89th Street. For many years the monument was the destination of the city's Memorial Day parade up Riverside Drive. Today, the ensemble, in spite of being in serious need of restoration, remains a particularly dignified and impressive one—beautifully set, scaled, and detailed.

173–175 Riverside Drive (1925–1926) gracefully follows the curve of the Drive between 89th and 90th Streets. The building, erected in two sections, is a characteristically suave performance by apartment house specialist J. E. R. Carpenter. There is appealingly understated Gothic detailing and an effective chamfered corner at 89th Street. The building replaced two mansions owned by members of the Clark family, who were pioneers in the development of the Upper West Side. Babe Ruth lived here in the early 1940s. The facade of **180 Riverside Drive** next door also gracefully follows the road's curve.

Figure 6.12. 180 Riverside Drive.

Just north of 91st Street Riverside Drive splits into two parts: a principal four-lane lower roadway and a separate upper access road onto which the apartment buildings in these blocks face. A narrow stretch of park separates the two streets. Olmsted employed this arrangement at several steeply sloping locations along the drive. Nearby, nestled down the slope on the promenade inside Riverside Park near the popular Hippo Playground (there is also a Dinosaur Playground at 96th Street) is the **91st Street Garden**, a long-running community effort that is very much worth a visit.

The apartment buildings between 91st and 95th Streets along the upper section of Riverside Drive tend to be older than those to the south. Some, like **190 Riverside** (1909–1910; Townsend, Steinle & Haskell) or **194 Riverside** (1902; Ralph Townsend), are organized around deep courtyards and feature richly sculptural decorative embellishments in stone and terracotta. The wide alleyway between the buildings was once a lane that connected to the Bloomingdale Road to the east.

At 93rd Street Anna Hyatt Huntington's statue of **Joan of Arc** occupies a protected site between the two roadways.

Figure 6.13. Joan of Arc monument.

The heroic figure dates to 1915 and sits on a base by John V. Van Pelt. The fifteenth-century heroine, who inspired the French in their efforts to shake off English rule, enjoyed a particular vogue in the early years of the twentieth century thanks to a novel by Mark Twain, a play by George Bernard Shaw, and a celebrated silent film. In New York a committee to erect a monument to the saint on the 500th anniversary of her birth had been formed in 1909. Based on a model she exhibited at the Paris Salon of 1910, Huntington was awarded the commission. Her figure of Joan in armor, sword in hand, rising in her stirrups and looking skyward, signals the heroine's nationalist and religious fervor. The Gothic arched pedestal actually contains stone fragments from the cell in Rouen where Joan was imprisoned before her execution, as well as a bit of Reims Cathedral. The striking monument, unveiled during World War I, depicting a female hero sculpted by a female artist, created a sensation and launched Huntington's career. So popular was the work that replicas were soon erected in Quebec City; Gloucester, Massachusetts; Blois, France; and Lincoln Park, San Francisco.

Up ahead, Riverside Drive passes on a viaduct over West 96th Street, which itself dives down to provide a connection to the Henry Hudson Parkway. There is a set of clay surface tennis courts at river level. The courts occupy the former site of a group of coal piers.

On the northeast corner of 96th Street the **Cliff Dwelling** at 243 Riverside (1914–1916; Herman Lee Meader) is one of New York's most idiosyncratic apartment houses. The developer had hoped to acquire multiple parcels of land on the block. When his efforts failed, he went ahead and built on the shallow triangle he was able to purchase. Of necessity, all the rooms face either onto 96th Street or Riverside Drive, and as the building's northern tip is barely nine feet wide, apartment layouts are beyond awkward. The Cliff Dwelling was originally an apartment hotel offering small one- or two-bedroom suites and an in-house restaurant on the mezzanine level. When the building became a co-op in 1979, most of the original units were combined to form larger, more livable apartments.

The architect, who lived for a time in the old Waldorf Hotel, was equally famous for his lively parties and for his enthusiasm for Mexico. He incorporated Mexican elements in several of his buildings, and they are the real glory of the Cliff Dwelling. The exterior of the 12-story yellow brick building is decorated with spirited Mayan, Aztec, and Native American motifs in terracotta, streamlined to conform to the style of the building's spirited Art Deco lobby.

Figure 6.14. The Cliff Dwelling.

The blocks between 96th and 110th Streets are the heart of the Bloomingdale neighborhood, the largest of the series of old villages that once dotted the highlands on the west side of Manhattan Island. Riverside Drive splits again at 97th Street. The upper roadway leads past 258 Riverside, the **Peter Stuyvesant** (1908–1909; William L. Rouse). The building has lost both its cornice and its original balconies, but the elegant terracotta detailing on the top two floors remains intact. **260 Riverside** across the street is a close relative, designed by the same architect during the same years.

Across the street, just inside the park between 98th and 99th Streets, is the **John Merven Carrère Memorial**. The terrace, balustrade, and staircase are the work of Carrère's partner Thomas Hastings, with whom he designed the New York Public Library and other major New York landmarks. Paid for by a group of the architect's friends, the memorial was presented to the city in 1919.

At 100th Street the upper and lower roadways frame the **New York Firemen's Memorial** (1913; Attilio Piccirilli, sculptor; H. Van Buren Magonigle, architect; restored 1987–1992). The memorial was created at the initiative of Episcopal Bishop Henry C. Potter and Macy's Department Store owner Isidor Straus, who lived nearby. Originally intended for Union Square, the complex includes a staircase, a terrace, and a fountain, as well as the monument itself. The bronze relief depicts horses drawing an engine to a fire while the flanking statues allegorically represent duty and sacrifice. The memorial continues to be the focus of an annual commemoration honoring firefighters who have lost their lives in the line of duty.

After a series of apartment blocks designed by Rouse & Goldstone, George Pelham, and Rosario Candela, the upper roadway passes a small group of surviving townhouses. **Numbers 292 and 293** were erected in 1896–1897 to designs by C. P. H. Gilbert. They are a handsome if unremarkable pair dominated by bold curving bays that extend all the way down to an English basement.

The landmarked **William and Clara Baumgarten House** next door at 294 Riverside Drive (1900–1901; Schickel & Ditmars) is more individual in character. A graceful Ionic portico, rusticated ground floor, fine ironwork balconies, bold Beaux Arts stone detailing, and a mansard roof with distinctive dormers combine to form a spirited composition. The builder of the house, William Baumgarten, was a furniture and interior designer who headed the celebrated firm of Herter Brothers before establishing his own business. Architect William Schickel regularly worked for both Herter Brothers and Baumgarten, so it is not unreasonable to assume that the design of 294 Riverside Drive was a collaborative effort.

The **Master Building** at 310 Riverside; (1928–1929; Harvey Wiley Corbett) was conceived as a hotel with an artistic mission. The 29-story Art Deco tower was commissioned by financier Louis Horch as a center for art education and as the New York base for the Russian artist and theosophist Nicholas Roerich (1874–1947) of whom Horch was a generous patron. In addition to 390 small apartments and a restaurant, the building contained on its lower floors the Master Institute, composed of a 300-seat theater, a museum devoted to Roerich's work, an art library, and studio space. Horch saw the project as both a real estate investment and an educational opportunity—a place where artistic practice, spirituality, and daily life would coexist.

The lower floors offer a ceremonial entrance to the former museum facing Riverside Drive. On 103rd Street there are separate entrances to the theater and to the apartments. Above, the freestanding apartment tower

Figure 6.15. The Master Building.

is set back from the lot line on the north and east to achieve maximum architectural drama and to ensure that all the apartments enjoy light and air. The overall emphasis is strongly vertical. The building rises through a solid midsection to a richly complex crown with multiple setbacks, chamfered corners, and a distinctive cupola. Along the way the color of the carefully patterned brick modulates from deep purple to pale gray. The Master Building was also among the first in New York to make use of wraparound corner windows above cantilevered floor slabs. Impressively sited, dramatically massed, and carefully detailed, the Master Building is one of New York's Art Deco landmarks, a close relative of Corbett's other great skyscraper hotel at 1 Fifth Avenue.

The ambitious Master Institute quickly ran into financial difficulties. Horch took sole control of the building in 1932 and subsequently broke with Roerich. The former Roerich Museum was renamed the Riverside Museum and carried on until 1971, exhibiting the work of contemporary American artists. Today the tower is a cooperative, and a separate Roerich Museum occupies a townhouse on West 107th Street.

Clearly the architects of **315 Riverside Drive** (1930; Boak & Paris) were paying attention to what was happening next door. In terms of massing, materials, and setback line, the buildings are a handsome pair. 315 Riverside, however, is a bit less stylish. It is less insistently vertical in its articulation, lacks corner windows, uses a single-color brick laid in a simplified pattern, and has a less prepossessing entry.

The block between 105th and 106th Streets on Riverside Drive forms the core of a small historic district, nearly a full block of well-preserved townhouses from the turn of the twentieth century. Four of the finest houses were developed by Joseph A. Farley to designs by Janes & Leo.

330 Riverside (1901–1902; Janes & Leo) is a grand Parisian mansion transported to Manhattan. Buff brick plays off effectively against carved limestone. There are richly embellished brackets, balustrades and window pediments, a substantial mansard with dormers, and bold corner quoins. The entrance on 105th Street is highlighted by a projecting three-story vertical bay. Built on speculation, the house was purchased by Robert Benson Davis of the

Figure 6.16. 330 Riverside Drive.

Davis Baking Powder Company. Today the building is home to the Roman Catholic organization Opus Dei, which has beautifully restored the mansion.

Numbers **331 and 333 Riverside** were developed at the same time and feature similar detailing. The two buildings are near twins and were originally part of a trio. In 1963 a matching house at 332 Riverside was demolished by the American Buddhist Study Center. The original house was replaced by a very modest contemporary structure. A stern bronze statue of Buddhist monk Shinran-Shonin (1173–1262) stands out front. The figure, cast in the 1930s, long occupied a hillside overlooking Hiroshima, Japan. Miraculously, it survived the atomic blast and was relocated here in 1955.

Historically, number 331 is perhaps best known as the house that William Randolph Hearst bought for his mistress Marian Davies. Duke Ellington lived two doors down at 333 during his final years, and today 106th Street has been named in the band leader's honor. The next three houses, built in 1901–1902, are the work of Hoppin & Koen. Although each is distinctly and differently detailed, the architects have been careful to coordinate cornice heights and fenestration patterns to create a coherent group.

The row concludes at the corner of 106th Street with **River Mansion** at 337 Riverside Drive (1900–1902; Robert Kohn).

Figure 6.17. River Mansion.

Built of dark red brick with heavy contrasting limestone trim and a mansard crowded with dormers, the building has a somewhat forbidding aspect. The entrance, hunkering down under a heavy portico with its elaborate banded columns and the mansion's name emblazoned on a cartouche over the door, is undeniably impressive. Like the other homes nearby, River Mansion has a history of colorful and controversial owners. For details on the history of the block, see Daniel J. Watkin's *The Man with the Sawed-Off Leg and Other Tales of a New York City Block* (Arcade, 2018).

At the western end of 106th Street, Civil War **General Franz Sigel** sits astride his mount, gazing over Riverside Park to the Hudson River. The monument (1907) is the work of sculptor Karl Bitter, who made something of a specialty across New York of portraits of foreign-born American heroes. He executed likenesses of the Marquis de Lafayette, Baron Von Steuben, and Carl Schurz. Sigel, his subject here, was a German émigré who worked as a teacher and journalist before leading a regiment during the Civil War. In later life Sigel was active in New York politics and publishing. He even produced a design for an elevated railway.

Just down the hill, tucked into Riverside Park is the **Peter J. Sharp Volunteer House** (2006; Murphy, Burnham & Buttrick). The building started its life as a toolshed but has been handsomely enlarged and updated into a training and meeting space for park volunteers. Built on a steep slope, one enters the building from a bridge at the upper level into an elevated space wrapped with tall casement windows. The effect is much like being in a tree house. The western facade is balanced but asymmetrical, recalling the style of the Vienna Secession. Slightly to the south, on a terrace overlooking a series of sports fields, is a popular seasonal restaurant.

The gleaming white marble chateau at 351 Riverside Drive on the corner of 107th Street is the **Morris and Laurette Schinasi House** (1907–1909; William B. Tuthill).

Built for an American Ottoman cigarette manufacturer, the building is one of only two freestanding houses remaining on Riverside Drive. Morris's brother, Solomon, long occupied the other, the Isaac L. Rice House at 89th Street. Tuthill, best known as the architect of Carnegie Hall, provided his client with an eye-catching and carefully detailed French Renaissance home dominated by the tall, green-tiled mansard and elaborate dormers. The cool, self-contained mansion is set off from its surroundings not only by its material but by what is effectively a moat, providing light to the English basement. The house remains a private residence.

Figure 6.18. Morris and Laurette Schinasi House.

Next door, **352 and 353 Riverside** are twins, developed between 1899 and 1901 by silk merchant Adolphe Openhym and designed by Robert D. Kohn. Openhym and his family occupied the southern house, which remains a single-family home. Before being subdivided, the northern house was long the residence of financier William Clark Poillon. Happily, little has been done to change the exterior of either building.

At 110th Street we leave Bloomingdale and enter a new neighborhood: Morningside Heights.

7

110th Street to 153rd Street

110th Street (also known as Cathedral Parkway) marks the southern boundary of Morningside Heights, the first in a series of distinct hilltop neighborhoods that overlook the Hudson River in northern Manhattan. Each is separated from the next by a narrow valley. These natural geological depressions remain important links between the river and the interior of Manhattan Island.

Morningside Heights is best known as the home of half a dozen educational institutions: Columbia University, Barnard College, Teachers' College, the Manhattan School of Music, and the Union and Jewish Theological seminaries. The Cathedral of St. John the Divine, Riverside Church, and Grant's Tomb are here as well. Many of these institutions relocated to this once remote hilltop around the turn of the twentieth century, establishing Morningside Heights as New York's would-be acropolis.

The possibilities offered by Morningside Heights' dominant position overlooking the river were appreciated a century and a half ago. In 1880 President Ulysses S. Grant proposed it as the site for a world's fair. This idea was revived again in 1892 as part of New York's unsuccessful bid to host the World's Columbian Exposition. The grandest plan, however, was put forward by Cornelius Vanderbilt in 1909: a mammoth memorial to honor both Robert Fulton on the 100th anniversary of the launch of his steamship *Clermont* and Hendrik Hudson on the 300th anniversary of his "discovery" of the river that bears his name. Planned to stretch from 114th to 116th Streets, the memorial was to include Fulton's tomb, a naval museum, docks, promenades, and a reception hall where distinguished visitors would be welcomed to the city. The enormous undertaking never gained traction. An 18-day commemoration of the twin anniversaries, however, went ahead.

Figure 7.1. Map 7.

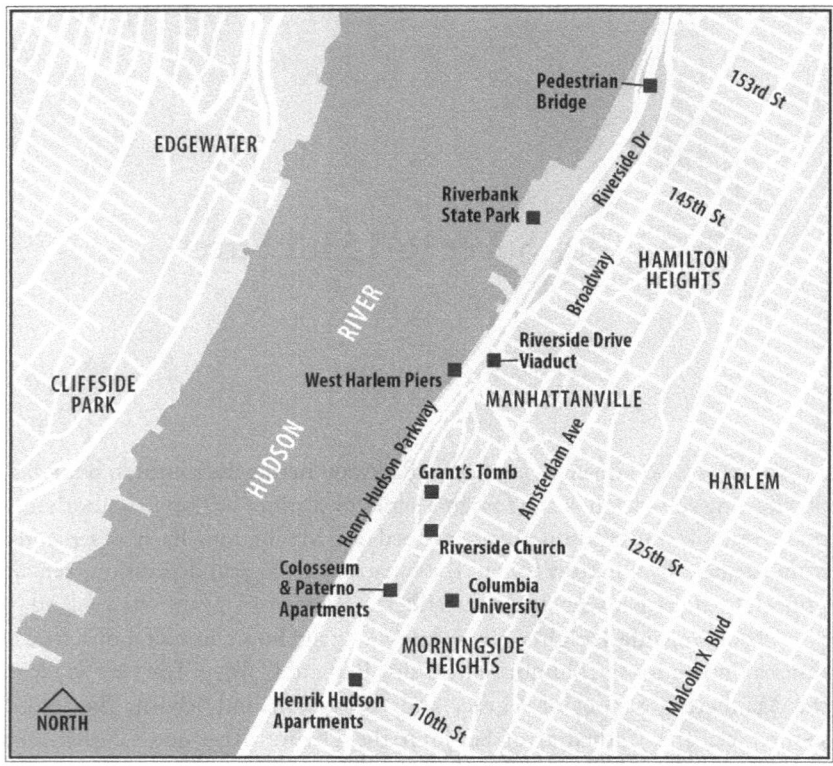

The **Hudson-Fulton Celebration** was a major event. There was an elaborate historic pageant downtown and an 800-boat naval parade on the Hudson, including not just war ships but replicas of Hudson's *Half Moon* and Fulton's *Clermont*. Over a million people watched from Riverside Park as the two ships collided mid-river. Wilbur Wright's 33-minute flight up the river and around Grant's Tomb proceeded without incident.

The Hudson-Fulton Celebration was in many ways a turning point. On one hand, it marked a high point of civic appreciation for the beauty, history, and cultural importance of the river. On the other hand, the celebration signaled the beginning of a fundamental shift in the relationship between the Hudson and the communities on its shores. Within months the first railway tunnel under the river opened for service. In the coming decades additional rail and road tunnels would be pushed beneath the water, bridges would be built to span the river, and channels would be dredged to accommodate increasingly large ships. As cities and industry along the Hudson grew, increasing quantities of untreated sewage and other waste were dumped directly into the river. Stench and disease became a significant problem. Fish populations plummeted, and in 1916 a typhoid epidemic forced the closing of the river's long-celebrated oyster beds. It was not until the passage of the federal Clean Water Act in 1972 that meaningful positive change began.

From 110th Street to 125th Street the best walking route north lies along Riverside Drive. Unlike the stretches of the boulevard to the south, few private mansions were erected north of 110th Street. Residential construction here, on high ground close to several parks, was spurred by ongoing nearby institutional development and by the completion in 1904 of the Interborough Rapid Transit (IRT) subway under Broadway. Large apartment buildings rose quickly on the blocks of Riverside Drive north of 110th Street. Among the most spectacular is the **Hendrik Hudson**, 380 Riverside Drive.

Figure 7.2. Hendrik Hudson apartments.

Completed in 1907 to designs by William Rouse, the building, designed to resemble an oversize Tuscan villa, was among the largest in the city at the time of its completion. Carefully planned to take full advantage of park and river views, the building was a showpiece. From the Baroque caryatid-flanked entrance on 110th Street (inspired by that of the city hall in Toulon, France), to the rhythmically placed balconies, elaborate terra-cotta decoration, and Palladian-arched rooftop belvederes, the building was designed to impress. Unfortunately, time has not been kind to the Hendrik Hudson. A rooftop pergola between the towers, as well as the original broad red-tiled eaves and sections of the tower pavilions themselves have all vanished. Inside, the once spacious apartments have been repeatedly subdivided. The splendid entry portal remains intact.

The **Samuel Tilden Monument** (1926; William Ordway Patridge) stands on Riverside Drive at 112th Street. A longtime reform leader of the New York Democratic Party, Tilden was celebrated for his challenges to the dominant Tweed Ring. He was elected governor in 1874 and ran for president two years later. In spite of attracting a majority of the popular vote, Tilden lost in the Electoral College to Rutherford B. Hayes. A highly successful attorney and dedicated book collector, Tilden is perhaps best remembered today as was one of the founders of the New York Public Library. Given his experience in the presidential election, one might well take the inscription on the monument's base, "I trust the people," to be either ironic or defiant. Before leaving 112th Street, look to the east for a view of the monumental facade of the Episcopal Cathedral of St. John the Divine.

400 Riverside Drive, **Fowler Court** (1909; George Pelham) is less grandiose than many of its neighbors but has a finely balanced facade of brick and limestone with well-placed bow windows. Next door, **The Strathmore** at 404 Riverside Drive (1910; Schwartz & Gross) is among the most handsome buildings in the neighborhood. It features a fine rusticated limestone base, a well-proportioned brick midsection, and a crown that retains its impressive cornice. The most dramatic feature of the building, however, is the entrance, flanked by majestic torchieres and protected by a graceful iron marquee (originally glazed). The building, which had only two apartments per floor when it was completed, has been subdivided but retains much of its original character.

At 113th Street the **Lajos (Louis) Kossuth Monument** commemorates the hero of the failed 1848 Hungarian revolution. To many Kossuth was a living embodiment of his nation's efforts to gain independence from Austria. The memorial is the work of Hungarian sculptor Janos Horvai

Figure 7.3. 404 Riverside Drive.

and was unveiled on March 15, 1928, Hungarian Independence Day. The monument includes not just the obligatory figure of Kossuth himself but an evocative tableau of a revolutionary soldier described as "liberating an aged peasant from poverty and oppression."

410 Riverside Drive (1910; Neville & Bagge) is the first in a long series of buildings along Riverside Drive owned by Columbia University (among New York's largest landlords) and used to provide house students, faculty, and administrators. The building's most distinguishing features are its covered porte-cochere and spikey Flemish gables.

St. Anthony Hall at 434 Riverside Drive (1898; Wood, Palmer & Hornbostel) was built as the home of the Delta Psi fraternity, which relocated here from their original premises on 28th Street when Columbia University moved north. The style of the group's imposing clubhouse, blending brick

Figure 7.4. 410 Riverside Drive.

and limestone, recalls both French Renaissance precedents and Charles McKim's two preferred materials for the buildings of the Columbia campus then rising nearby. The fraternity house is still in use, featuring a dining room, ballroom, billiard room, and study spaces. Henry Hornbostel, who practiced largely in Pittsburgh, is best known in New York for his distinctive designs for the Hellgate, the Manhattan, and the Queensboro Bridges over the East River.

Just north of St. Anthony Hall, 116th Street inclines steeply down the hill from the Columbia campus to Riverside Park. The broad intersection was originally planned as a ceremonial gathering place for processions moving between the proposed riverfront Fulton Memorial and Grant's Tomb. Today the intersection derives its drama from a pair of wonderfully complementary apartment buildings: **The Colosseum** (435 Riverside) and **The Paterno** (440 Riverside).

Figure 7.5. 440 Riverside Drive.

Both were built in 1910 by the prolific Paterno construction family to plans by Schwartz & Gross, who along with Neville & Bagge and Gaetan Ajello designed so many buildings in the neighborhood.

At the foot of 116th Street the facade of the Colosseum curves boldly to the south, while across the way The Paterno turns in the opposite direction, leading the eye northward to Claremont Avenue. The buildings are beautifully matched in materials and Renaissance-inspired detailing. Of the two, the smaller Colosseum was the more exclusive. The larger Paterno featured apartments organized around two internal courtyards. It has two entries, one a covered porte-cochere on Riverside Drive opening into a lobby with a handsome stained-glass ceiling, the other under the tower on Claremont Avenue. Alas, both buildings have lost their original cornices and several of their towers. Today The Paterno is a co-op; Columbia owns The Colosseum.

At the foot of 116th Street, just inside Riverside Park, there is a handsome bench and drinking fountain, erected in 1910 to commemorate the 25th anniversary of the founding of the **Women's Health Protection**

Association. The association was organized to focus attention on several pressing public health issues: water supply, street cleaning, garbage disposal, and school hygiene. The group was proactive and achieved significant results. Based on the success of the New York organization, chapters were founded in numerous other cities. The monument to their work was designed by Bruno Louis Zimm.

The block to the north of The Paterno along Riverside Drive is occupied by an impressive row of apartment houses dating to the first decade of the twentieth century. Nearly all are now owned by Columbia. 452 Riverside Drive, the **Mira Mar** (1909; Gaetan Ajello), is particularly appealing.

119th Street marks the start of a three-block stretch of Riverside Drive dominated by **Riverside Church** (1926–1930; Henry C. Pelton with Allen

Figure 7.6. Riverside Church.

& Collens) and its associated buildings. The church complex is the result of a partnership between John D. Rockefeller Jr. and the charismatic pastor of the Park Avenue Baptist Church, Harry Emerson Fosdick. Both were interested in creating a new type of interdenominational church that would offer a diverse range of worship options for a variety of constituencies. The result is New York's most impressive skyscraper church. The building is anchored by a 392-foot Gothic tower containing 21 floors of church offices and an powerful 74-bell carillon, once the largest in the world. Compared to the enormous tower, the adjoining church, with its broad, low nave seating a full 2,400 worshippers, seems almost an afterthought. The complex was funded entirely by Rockefeller, who did so much for the natural and cultural landscape of northern Manhattan. It includes a school, gymnasium, theater, and offices for the church's ambitious social welfare programs. Additional buildings of less architectural interest have subsequently been added to the complex. These include the church's **Martin Luther King Jr. Wing** (1959) to the south and the large, bland **Interchurch Center** (1956–1958; Voorhees, Walker, Smith, Smith & Haines with Collens, Willis & Beckonert) between 119th and 120th Streets.

The collegiate Gothic buildings of the **Union Theological Seminary** (1906; Allen & Collens) stand just to the east of Riverside Church. In search of additional revenue, the seminary recently commissioned a 41-story apartment tower for its courtyard. The handsome new building, dubbed **Claremont Hall** (2023; RAMSA), soars over the original complex and even over the neighboring tower of Riverside Church. Clad in gray brick and textured precast concrete to mimic the stone of the original seminary buildings, the tower includes both apartments and classroom space. The former refectory has become a swimming pool. Taken together the Claremont and Riverside Church towers are the most prominent landmarks on the Hudson River shoreline between Midtown and the George Washington Bridge.

Just to the north, across 122nd Street, **Sakura (Cherry Blossom) Park** honors Japan's gift of 2,000 cherry trees to New York City in conjunction with the 1909 Hudson-Fulton Celebration. Unfortunately, the ship carrying the initial consignment of trees was lost at sea, so a second shipment was required. It arrived four years later. The trees were eventually planted in two groups. One was set along the banks of the Hudson from 100th to 125th Streets (the Cherry Walk). The second was placed here in Sakura Park. The current appearance of the park is the result of an Olmsted Brothers–designed update in 1932 funded by John D. Rockefeller Jr. A second update in 1981 added additional plantings and a small pavilion,

Figure 7.7. Claremont Hall.

often put to good use by students from the nearby Manhattan School of Music. The statue at the southern end of the park honors Civil War General Daniel Butterfield. The monument was erected in 1918 and is the work of Gutzon Borglum of Mount Rushmore fame. In addition to his military accomplishments, Butterfield is known as the composer of Taps and as a founder of the American Express company.

The plain, dignified stone buildings of the **Manhattan School of Music** (1910; Donn Barber; 1931 addition by Shreve, Lamb & Harmon) sit just to the east of Sakura Park. The Manhattan School moved to this limestone block in 1969 when the Julliard School, the former occupant of the site, relocated to Lincoln Center.

The northern boundary of Sakura Park is marked by the large, symmetrical, and architecturally understated **International House** (1924; Lindsay & Warren), a residence for international students at the various schools in Morningside Heights. Funding came once again from John D. Rockefeller Jr., who was inspired to create an institution to foster international peace and understanding in the wake of World War I. Although the design of the exterior of the building was based on that of Italian Renaissance villas, the interiors were decorated, at Mrs. Rockefeller's insistence, in an American Colonial style.

To the west, the two lanes of Riverside Drive separate to enclose the imposing **General Grant National Memorial** (1891–1897; John Duncan).

New York beat out stiff competition to become the final resting place of the 18th president. This massive and somber granite structure is the result. The tomb of another soldier and national leader, Napoleon, was clearly the

Figure 7.8. General Grant National Memorial.

architect's inspiration, although Duncan's design is also heavily indebted to the ancient Greek mausoleum at Halicarnassus. Inside, beyond the stern Doric portico and under the enormous dome, are the twin polished granite sarcophagi of General and Mrs. Ulysses S. Grant. On the walls, sculptural reliefs and mosaics depict major events in Grant's life. The two eagles out front were moved here from New York's old central post office near City Hall in the 1930s during a renovation. There is a visitor center just to the east, under a pergola-covered overlook. Once the most visited attraction in New York City (the tomb's dedication drew a million spectators), today Grant's Tomb is often nearly deserted.

In 1974, the National Park Service commissioned artist Pedro Silva, assisted by a group of community volunteers, to create the ***Rolling Bench***, which flanks the memorial. It would be hard to imagine a less congenial pairing than the playful, undulating, Gaudi-inspired mosaic benches and the self-conscious formality of the memorial.

Just to the west of the memorial, hidden in a grove of trees overlooking the park and the river, is the modest and poignant **Amiable Child Monument**.

Figure 7.9. Amiable Child Monument.

The inscription on the base reads "Erected to the memory of an Amiable Child, St. Claire Pollack, Died 15 July 1797 in the Fifth Year of His Age." St. Claire was the son of George and Catherine Pollock, prosperous linen merchants who had a summer home on the knoll just north of the site of Grant's Tomb. Wandering away from his nurse, St. Claire fell from the nearby cliffs. The Pollocks moved away, and in the middle years of the nineteenth century their cottage was expanded and converted into the **Claremont Inn**. With the construction of Riverside Park, the city took control of the property but leased it back to a succession of operators. The inn was long a popular gathering place for celebrities and politicians. It continued to operate through prohibition before ultimately expiring in a fire in 1951. A playground with a commemorative plaque occupies the site today.

The Claremont Inn originally marked the northern terminus of Riverside Drive. But in 1897, the state legislature voted to extend it northward to 157th Street. Geography, however, was a problem. Just north of 122nd Street the land drops away sharply as Morningside Heights gives way to a natural valley. The solution was a 2,000-foot **viaduct** bridging the gap and carrying Riverside Drive north to 135th Street.

Figure 7.10. Manhattanville Viaduct.

To get a proper view of this elegant piece of engineering, walk down the **St. Clair Stairs** on the left just before the spot where the two lanes of Riverside Drive recombine to travel across the viaduct. From the foot of the stairs there is a dramatic view northward through the 26 decorative steel arches of the 80-foot-tall trestle. The viaduct was completed in 1900 to designs by F. Stuart Williamson. He is also responsible for a number of the impressive embankments, stairs, and stone terraces that we will encounter farther north in Riverside Park.

Standing under the viaduct it quickly becomes obvious that the rigid grid that normally controls Manhattan's street layout breaks apart here. For example, 125th Street runs at a distinct angle to intersect with 130th Street near the river. This is the legacy of **Manhattanville**, the old community spanned by the viaduct. Laid out before the city's grid plan was adopted, Manhattanville sits in the valley between Morningside and Hamilton Heights and is one of only a few places in upper Manhattan offering easy access to the banks of the Hudson from the center of the island. A Dutch community developed here in the seventeenth century, and during the Revolutionary War the valley, known then as the Hollow Way, was the center of the Battle of Harlem Heights.

In the nineteenth century, Manhattanville developed as a major transportation center. A ferry to New Jersey was in operation by 1808, and in 1850 the new Hudson River Railroad built a station here. Riverboat and rail connections soon made Manhattanville not just a popular retreat for downtown dwellers but also a natural spot for the development of commerce and industry. The valley would long be an important depot for construction materials as well as the site of dairies, breweries, and automobile plants.

Today the neighborhood is dominated by the newly developed **Manhattanville Campus of Columbia University**, including the Jerome L. Green Science Center and the Lenfest Center for the Arts housed in sleek buildings by Renzo Piano. A new home for the Columbia Business School (2023; Diller Scofidio + Renfro with FXCollaborative) is located immediately to the east of the viaduct. The showy business school campus is composed of two large towers that house classrooms, offices, a library, and living spaces. The towers are separated by a public park. In developing the area, Columbia, after decades of mutual town-gown suspicion and sometimes hostility, has worked hard to create spaces where the local and university communities can meet and interact.

To the west, beyond the Riverside Drive viaduct and Henry Hudson Parkway, the river frontage has been handsomely redeveloped as the **West**

Figure 7.11. Henry R. Kravis Hall, Columbia University Business School.

Harlem Piers. These blocks were once largely given over to commercial wharfs and a ferry slip. Until the 1930s boats ran regularly from here to New Jersey and to Coney Island. A large recreation pier was built at the foot of what is now St. Clair Place in 1897. It featured facilities for river bathing, concerts, and dining. That pier survived until 1965. A second pier nearby was, until 1971, a stop for the celebrated Hudson River Day Line, providing service to the Catskills, Bear Mountain, and points north.

The current sliver of a park with its distinctive sharply angled piers opened in 2008. It was designed by W. Architecture & Landscape Architecture and includes facilities for kayak launching, fishing, river watching, and small concerts. The park is also home to the *Baylander*, a former US Navy helicopter landing training ship that since 2020 has been anchored here each summer as a floating restaurant. Scattered through the park are stainless steel sculptures by artist Nari Ward along with intriguing signs mounted on sections of highway guardrail that poetically link neighborhood street names with weather conditions and bucolic sounds. The Hudson River Greenway skirts the east side of the park along what is appropriately known as Marginal Street.

In spite of the various bridges and viaducts that compete for attention here, it is impossible not to notice that the railway has made a reappearance. The tracks emerge from their long tunnel under Riverside Park at 124th Street to run in the open all the way to the Spuyten Duyvil bridge. Amtrak trains are a frequent presence along the banks of the river and in the northern sequence of parks.

From the West Harlem Piers, 12th Avenue runs directly under the Riverside Drive viaduct, passing an abandoned city garbage transfer station in the river and some gritty and evocative warehouses. At 135th Street a serviceable stone stair leads back up from water level to Riverside Drive.

Not far from the northern end of the Riverside Drive viaduct is the wonderfully incongruous classical facade of the **Lee Brothers Storage Building** (now Manhattan Mini Storage) at 570 Riverside Drive. Erected in 1927 to designs by Chicago architect George Kingsley. The facade features particularly fine terracotta detailing and presents a dignified face to the river. Behind the storage building looms the mammoth octagonal **Riverside Park Community** public housing complex (1976; Richard Dattner & Associates).

135th Street marks the beginning of a new neighborhood. This is **Hamilton Heights**, named for Alexander Hamilton, whose home, The Grange, lies a few blocks to the east. Most of the apartment buildings here are modest in their ambitions and date to the years immediately following the opening of the IRT subway in 1904. Typically, they are so-called New Law Tenements. Six stories in height, organized around central courtyards, and often exuberantly decorated, the buildings conform to the strict requirements of the New York State Tenement House Act of 1901.

A little farther along at 630 Riverside Drive, the **Academy of the Holy Child** (1911; John W. Kearney) is a somewhat forbidding edifice. Built as a Catholic girl's school and later known as St. Walburga's Academy, the building is currently the home of the Fortune Academy, which provides housing and services for previously incarcerated individuals.

Back to the south at 138th Street is a bridge leading over the highway and the railway to **Riverbank State Park** (Dattner Architects with Abel Bainnson Butz Landscape Architects) running from 137th to 145th Streets.

The park is one of only three in the city administered by the State of New York. It offers 28 acres of recreational facilities perched on top of New York's largest sewage treatment facility.

Figure 7.12. Riverbank State Park. *Source:* Alamy.

Historically, the bulk of Manhattan's sewage was discharged directly into the Hudson. The resulting environmental and public health issues were recognized, but the questions of where to locate an appropriate treatment plant and how to pay for it remained long unresolved. Federal funds to support construction became available in 1965, but the question of where to locate a plant large enough to treat hundreds of millions of gallons of wastewater a day remained vexing. The present site was a leading choice, but the residents of Hamilton Heights and West Harlem were understandably skeptical of plans to locate the plant in their neighborhood. The decision, inspired by Japanese examples, to place a large park on the facility's roof was key to securing neighborhood acceptance of the project.

Concrete caissons to support the treatment plant were sunk in the river beginning in 1972, and after frequent construction delays and numerous design changes, the plant finally began to treat waste in 1986. The North River Wastewater Treatment Plant today handles all of the sewage generated in Manhattan west of Fifth Avenue and north of Bank Street. The facility's understated external appearance nods to both the work of Louis Kahn and to the arches of Roman aqueducts: rows of semicircular arches set within square concrete panels and enlivened with occasional touches of color.

While the sewage plant itself was under construction, wrangling about the design of the rooftop park continued. Initial designs by Philip Johnson, Gruzen Architects, Bond Ryder Associates, and Lawrence Halprin were all rejected, and in 1980 Richard Dattner was finally chosen as the park's designer. After compromises resulting from the structural limitations of the supporting sewage plant and constantly shrinking budgets, the park opened to near universal acclaim in 1993. Amenities include an Olympic-sized swimming pool, a roller- and ice-skating rink, a 400-meter track, gyms, tennis courts, soccer fields, a restaurant, and ample strolling and picnic areas. There is also a carousel and a small river-level amphitheater with expansive views.

Not surprisingly, odor was initially a problem, but after some rancorous protests, a good deal of obfuscation, and some engineering upgrades this was eventually sorted out. Today it is possible to enjoy the carefully laid-out facilities of Riverside Park, along with the great views up and down the river from the perimeter promenade, nearly unaware of what is happening beneath one's feet.

At the north end of Riverbank State Park a spiral staircase leads back down to river level and to a series of sports fields built on landfill. Here the Hudson River Greenway follows a gracious tree-flanked *allée* along the river.

Figure 7.13. View north from Riverbank State Park.

At 152nd Street there is a new (2017) **pedestrian bridge** over the highway and railway.

Named in honor of New York Assemblyman Herman "Denny" Farrell, the $27 million project includes not just a gracefully arched truss bridge over the roadways but also what must be one of the most complex series of access ramps in the city. Space on both sides of the bridge was limited, so designers had to be creative in squeezing in their switchbacks. The integration of the ramps with the existing restored stone bastion off Riverside Drive is particularly impressive.

For a short diversion, cross over the bridge. At its eastern end, on Riverside Drive and 150th Street, is artist Elizabeth Catlett's **Ralph Ellison Memoria**l.

The sculpture, erected in 2003, features a large bronze slab containing a cutout silhouette figure—a reference to the author's most famous novel, *Invisible Man*. Ellison lived for many years nearby at 730 Riverside Drive, a building that was also at one time home to singer Marian Anderson and to US Senator Jacob Javits.

Between 153rd Street and 161st Street, Riverside Drive travels along yet another viaduct, spanning the valley that separates Hamilton Heights from Washington Heights. Our route north follows the riverside pathway that runs underneath.

Figure 7.14. Denny Farrell Greenway Bridge.

Figure 7.15. Ralph Ellison Memorial.

8

153rd Street to Spuyten Duyvil

This walk will take us from the former home of naturalist John James Audubon to the majestic span of the George Washington Bridge, and then northward beneath the riverside cliffs through Washington Heights to Inwood at the northern tip of Manhattan.

At 153rd Street the terrain slopes down to another natural valley. Here in 1841 Trinity Church purchased 23-acres as the site for a new cemetery because its own churchyard on lower Broadway was filled to capacity. James Renwick laid out the new burial ground as a handsome park with lovely views, gentle terraces, and walkways for strolling. A pier on the river offered easy access to the cemetery by boat from downtown. **Trinity Church Cemetery** is today the only active burial ground in Manhattan and houses the remains of such notables as John Jacob Astor, Ralph Ellison, and Ed Koch.

One year later, in 1842, John James Audubon acquired a 14-acre plot of farmland just to the north and built a family home. It was here that he produced his celebrated magnum opus *Birds of America*. After Audubon's death the farm became known as Minnie's Land, after the author's nickname for his wife. Today Minnie's Land is the site of the **Audubon Park Historic District**. (The naturalist himself is buried nearby in the Trinity Cemetery.) The neighborhood was planned as a discrete upscale enclave and was constructed in large part between 1905 and 1910. Its tall, architecturally ambitious apartment houses are arranged on irregular, curving streets that defy the Manhattan grid to create a distinct sense of place.

Audubon Park is also the home of **Audubon Terrace**, an ambitious project erected by arts patron Archer Huntington in the early years of the

Figure 8.1. Map 8.

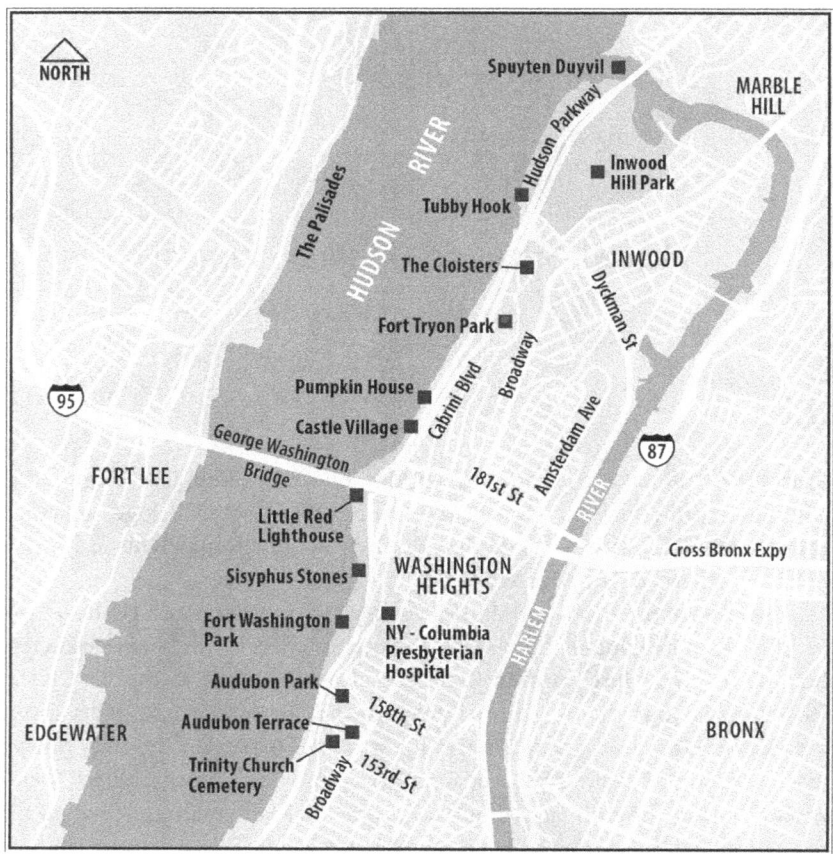

twentieth century to provide a consolidated home for several of the museums and learned societies that he supported. The American Numismatic Society, American Geographic Society, Museum of the American Indian, American Academy of Arts and Letters, and the Hispanic Society were all originally housed here in buildings grouped around an elevated plaza. Today, most of these organizations have relocated. Only the Hispanic Society and Academy remain active on Audubon Terrace.

Today, the main route of Riverside Drive runs just to the west of both the cemetery and Audubon Park on a raised viaduct over the low-lying riverbank. This was not always the case. As in Manhattanville to the south, a viaduct was necessary to carry the drive over the valley at 153rd Street.

Figure 8.2. Trinity Cemetery.

Initially, however, Trinity Church refused to cede the necessary land at the western end of its property. This disappointed the developers of nearby Audubon Park, who would have liked nothing better than for fashionable Riverside Drive to be extended to the new neighborhood.

It took until 1908, but a complicated agreement was ultimately worked out, one that continues to breed confusion to this day. A cantilevered span carries Riverside Drive over the valley at the foot of the cemetery. At 155th Street the drive turns sharply to the northeast to cut a curving swath through Audubon Park until it reaches 158th Street. There it doubles back to the northwest to 161st Street, where it originally linked up with the Boulevard Lafayette, an unpaved drive running north from this point to Dyckman Street. Boulevard Lafayette was eventually upgraded and renamed to become part of the extended Riverside Drive.

Audubon Park developed quickly around this new stretch of Riverside Drive, but motorists traveling north soon began to complain about the curving detours through the neighborhood. These were eliminated in 1927 by the construction of an additional masonry viaduct that carried Riverside Drive directly northward between 155th and 161st Streets. As a result, there are now two roads in the neighborhood called Riverside Drive, a curving one to the east and a direct one to the west. No one wanted to give up their Riverside Drive address, and the confusing nomenclature remains in place.

Riverside Park officially ends at 155th Street. It is succeeded there by **Fort Washington Park,** named for the Revolutionary War redout on the heights above. The park, which runs along the river as far as Dyckman Street, was mapped in 1894 and slowly assembled by the city through eminent domain between 1896 and 1927. The initial section, extending as far north

Figure 8.3. Sutherland apartments, Audubon Park.

as the George Washington Bridge, is filled along the way with ball fields, picnic groves, and tennis courts.

Continuing north, things are a little gloomy at first. The riverside walkway runs beneath an elevated section of the Henry Hudson Parkway, and there is an emergency sewage overfall at 158th Street that can tend toward the pungent. Things pick up after that, and the path affords attractive views across the river to New Jersey. Communities along the far shore are divided between those at river level and those atop the increasingly tall Palisades. **Edgewater**, on the lower level, has grown rapidly in recent years, with apartment buildings replacing what was long an industrial landscape that included a huge Ford Motor Company assembly facility and an Alcoa aluminum plant.

On the cliffs above, Cliffside Park and Fort Lee were once the home of the 38-acre **Palisades Amusement Park**. The park operated from 1898 to 1971 and was among the nation's most popular, attracting at its peak six million annual visitors. It featured the world's largest saltwater swimming pool (with water piped up from the Hudson) and the celebrated Cyclone rollercoaster. In the 1960s Palisades Park held much the same place in the lives of young New Jersey residents as Coney Island did for New Yorkers.

In the early years of the twentieth century, **Fort Lee**, just to the north of Palisades Park, was the center of the American film industry. Beginning around 1909 such major movie pioneers as William Fox, Sam Goldwyn, Louis B. Mayer, and Adolf Zukor set up studios on the Palisades. Soon directors like D. W. Griffith and Mack Sennett were turning out films featuring Mary Pickford, Lillian Gish, Theda Bara, Douglas Fairbanks, and the Barrymores. Filming took place both in greenhouse-like studios and on the streets of the city. Although films continued to be made in Fort Lee until 1948, by the 1930s most of the studios had decamped to California in search of more predictable weather. The term cliffhanger, in which leading film characters find themselves in precarious situations from which they must extricate themselves, has its origins in Fort Lee, where many early stars found themselves filmed literally hanging over the cliffs above the Hudson. Today, Fort Lee is best known for being the western terminus of the George Washington Bridge and for having one of the largest Korean communities in the western hemisphere.

Back on the Manhattan side, the shore north of 165th Street is dominated by the enormous **New York Presbyterian–Columbia University Medical Center**. The hospital relocated to Washington Heights from midtown in the 1920s and commissioned architect James Gamble Rogers to design its new home. Over the years, the hospital campus has expanded dramatically to include clinics, staff apartments, and research buildings. From the park the most visible of these is the sleek **New York State Psychiatric Institute** (1998) by Ellerbe Becke. The building sits to the west of Riverside Drive in the midst of a spaghetti bowl of approach roadways to the George Washington Bridge. It is interesting to note that from 1903 to 1912 the hospital site was the location of Hilltop Park stadium, home to New York's American League baseball team—today known as the Yankees.

At river level this section of the Hudson shoreline is comparatively isolated from the city on the hills above. Between 145th and 181st Streets there are only two places to cross the highway and the railway to access Fort Washington Park. As a result, except on weekends, when the picnic areas attract large local crowds, the riverbank here feels quiet and set-apart. It's easy to get close to the river, to find a perch along the wooded shore from which to watch the water.

Near 170th Street the Hudson shoreline is occupied by the *Sisyphus Stones*.

In 2017 artist Uliks Gryka saw this rocky stretch of shoreline as a creative opportunity. He began to assemble stones of various sizes into carefully balanced figures and cairns. Soon the shore was lined with mute

Figure 8.4. *Sisyphus Stones.*

stone personages. The figures sometimes collapsed or were knocked down, but Gryka steadfastly rebuilt them and added more. Others joined in, and today, although Gryka himself has moved on, the shoreline is well populated by a constantly changing sequence of mysterious figures, mute and evocative.

The ancient-seeming assembly is doubly fascinating standing as it does in the shadow of the mighty **George Washington Bridge**. The idea for a bridge spanning the Hudson was first broached in 1888 and continued to be explored for the next 40 years. Early planning focused on a crossing at 59th Street, designed to carry both vehicular and railway traffic. A key issue from the start was how to design a bridge of sufficient height to allow large ships to pass underneath without requiring approach ramps that would of necessity extend halfway across Manhattan Island. The solution was to identify a site where there was high ground on both sides of the river. The ultimate choice was to connect Fort Lee, New Jersey, with 179th Street in Washington Heights, linking the Palisades with the former site of Fort Washington.

Figure 8.5. George Washington Bridge.

Plans for a bridge carrying only vehicular traffic (the planned addition of railway capacity was deemed too costly) were approved by the two state legislatures in 1923, and construction was entrusted to the newly created Port Authority of New York and New Jersey. Engineer Othmar Amman was hired to design the bridge with Cass Gilbert appointed as consulting architect. Construction began in 1927, and the bridge opened for traffic in 1931. Along the way, however, some major design changes took place. Initial plans called for the twin 570-foot towers supporting the bridge cables to be clad in masonry. Gilbert provided a streamlined classical design that included observation decks and a restaurant. The arrival of the Depression coincided with the scheduled start of work on the stone cladding; and with money in short supply it was decided to leave the handsome steel truss work of the towers unembellished. The decision has since been hailed as both an economic and aesthetic triumph, revealing and celebrating the powerful forms of the bridge's engineering. At the time of its completion the George Washington Bridge with a central span of 3,500 feet was the longest suspension bridge in the world, nearly twice the length of any previous crossing. Success was immediate, and a second deck was added to the bridge in 1962. Today, although it is no longer the world's longest suspension bridge, the George Washington Bridge is still the busiest, carrying 14 lanes of traffic.

In addition to providing access to northern Manhattan from New Jersey, the bridge is a key transportation link for the entire northeast. The completion of the Pennsylvania tunnels under the Hudson and East Rivers in 1910 and the construction of the New York Connecting Railway to the east in 1917 provided continuous rail access through Manhattan from points south to New England.

In 1927 the opening of the Holland Tunnel added the first direct vehicular access to Manhattan across the Hudson. The completion of the George Washington Bridge four years later was an even more significant step in ending Manhattan's island isolation and speeding its incorporation into a larger, unified metropolitan region. Although there are direct connections from the bridge to both city streets and to the Henry Hudson Parkway, much of the bridge's traffic continues across Manhattan in a 12-lane open cut (the Trans-Manhattan Expressway) to a bridge over the Harlem River and onward to the Cross Bronx Expressway and New England. This route, Interstate 95, is one of the Northeast's key commercial corridors.

The bridge is currently undergoing a major renovation and restoration, including cable replacement and painting. The project also includes new pedestrian and bicycle paths on both the north and south sides of the upper deck. The northern path is open and can be accessed from a handsome new entry at 189th Street and Cabrini Boulevard. The walk to Fort Lee offers stunning views up the Hudson as well as of the New Jersey and Manhattan shores. Along the way, the story of the bridge is told through informative illustrated text panels.

When designers were wrestling with exactly where to locate the George Washington Bridge, they took advantage of a bulge in the Manhattan shoreline at 178th Street, Jeffrey's Hook. This became the location of the bridge's eastern tower. Jeffrey's Hook had long been recognized as a danger to navigation, and by 1889 lanterns were regularly hung from poles there to warn mariners. These efforts proved inadequate, so in 1921 the US Coast Guard relocated an old lighthouse from Sandy Hook, New Jersey, to the site. The refurbished beacon served for 10 years until the lights on the newly opened bridge made it obsolete. The **Jeffrey's Hook Lighthouse** was officially decommissioned in 1948.

Figure 8.6. Jeffrey's Hook Lighthouse.

But that is not the end of the story. In 1942 authors Hildegarde Swift and Lynd Ward had published a children's book entitled *The Little Red Lighthouse and the Great Gray Bridge*. It tells the story of a tiny, plucky lighthouse holding its own against a much larger and somewhat haughty neighbor. The book was enormously popular; and when the Coast Guard proposed to auction off the lighthouse, a grassroots effort to save it was quickly organized. As a result, in 1951 the Coast Guard transferred ownership of the lighthouse to the New York City Parks Department, which cares for it today. A small red beacon still flashes in its tower.

Just north of the bridge our path turns inland. The route heads steeply uphill, crosses the railway line on a trestle, and passes under the southbound lane of the Henry Hudson Parkway to arrive at the base of Cass Gilbert's massive Manhattan anchorage for the George Washington Bridge. For the next 1.5 miles the path follows the route of the Hudson River Greenway, along the edge of the highway through narrow Fort Washington Park. This is the only stretch of the shoreline in Manhattan where it is impossible to walk along the Hudson's banks.

These blocks also mark an interruption in the route of Riverside Drive. Until the mid-1930s the drive extended all the way from 72nd Street to Dyckman Street as a graceful curving boulevard. When Robert Moses took over the redesign of Riverside Park, his plans included the continuation of the Henry Hudson Parkway all the way to the northern tip of Manhattan, across a new bridge, and on into the Bronx. To accomplish this, just north of the George Washington Bridge, Moses cut a new highway through the lower levels of Fort Washington Park to carry southbound traffic. For the northbound lane he simply appropriated Riverside Drive, converting it into a limited-access highway.

Riverside Drive thus disappears from the map altogether at 181st Street and only reappears very briefly again at Dyckman Street, where it turns eastward toward its original termination at Broadway.

(While the path along the highway is the most direct route north, a longer but more peaceful and scenic route is also available. It leads up through the Hudson Heights neighborhood and Fort Tryon Park before rejoining the river at Dyckman Street. This route is described below.)

Until the 1920s nearly all the land on the hills north of 181st Street was occupied by private estates. One of the most colorful residents was Charles Paterno. Paterno was an Italian immigrant who, with other members of his large family, created a highly successful real estate development firm that built well over 100 buildings on the Upper West Side and in Washington

Figure 8.7. View of Fort Washington Park from the George Washington Bridge.

Heights. Paterno was proud of his success, and between 1908 and 1916 he built himself a castle on the bluff at 183rd Street. The crenellated Gothic mansion boasting 35 rooms dominated the riverfront until 1938.

When Paterno moved into his castle, the surrounding neighborhood was largely undeveloped. He saw an opportunity. In 1923 he began work on a pioneering cooperative apartment complex, **Hudson View Gardens**, just east of his castle on the highest natural point in Manhattan. Designed as a Tudor village by architect George B. Pelham, the attractive complex was planned to appeal to families who might otherwise consider relocating to the suburbs.

In 1938 Paterno himself did just that, demolishing his castle and erecting **Castle Village**, a huge five-building complex of X-shaped buildings on his river-facing property.

The massive but timidly detailed red brick buildings were designed by Pelham's son, George F. Today the five towers dominate the shoreline north of the George Washington Bridge. Although Castle Village was intended for and continues to attract a middle-class clientele, the development's "tower in a park" plan was quickly adopted for many of the city's public housing

Figure 8.8. Castle Village.

projects. Perhaps the most dramatic event in the life of Castle Village occurred in May 2005, when the 75-foot retaining wall supporting the complex's garden collapsed onto the Henry Hudson Parkway below. Reconstruction took nearly five years.

At 186th Street, the so-called **Pumpkin House** looms precariously over the highway. The eccentric brick and concrete building was commissioned in 1925 by engineer Cleveland Walcutt, and its western facade does bear a striking resemblance to the face of a jack-o-lantern. The house stands on part of an estate once owned by James Gordon Bennett, the eccentric publisher of the *New York Herald*.

Originally, the **Inspiration Point Shelter** at 190th Street was a popular rest and viewing stop along Riverside Drive. Designed in 1924 by architect Gustave Steinacher, the handsome neoclassic pergola is today marooned, reachable only via the highway footpath. To the east, high on the cliff above the shelter, stands the **St. Frances Xavier Cabrini Shrine**. Mother Cabrini, who championed the cause of Italian immigrants in the United States, was the first naturalized American citizen canonized by the Roman Catholic Church. The shrine was built between 1957 and 1960 to designs by DeSina & Pellegrino and includes a mosaic cycle depicting key events in Cabrini's life. Although the saint's heart was sent to Rome, her preserved body is on view inside.

A few hundred yards further along, stone gates and an arched loggia on the east side of the highway mark the former Riverside Drive entrance to what was the estate of **Cornelius Kingsley Garrison Billings**. In 1901, Billings, a Chicago gas millionaire who loved horse racing, began construction

Figure 8.9. Loggia of the former Billings estate.

on what he called Fort Tryon Hall. The property eventually included not only a large house by architect Guy Lowell and a palatial stable block but also a curving brick carriage drive, an overlook terrace, a swimming pool, bowling alley, and a private yacht landing at Dyckman Street. The terrace and the estate gardener's cottage still stand high up on the hill.

Billings was serious about his love of horses. He raced regularly at the recently opened Harlem Speedway across the island, and in 1903 he staged a famous horseback dinner at Sherry's Restaurant in Midtown. Thirty-six guests dined in the restaurant's ballroom, each seated on their favorite mount.

In 1917 Billings sold his property to John D. Rockefeller Jr., who was at the time accumulating land in the area to create a public park. He soon added the adjacent estates of Walter S. Scheafer, William Henry Hays, and Jonas Libby to his parcel. In 1922 Rockefeller engaged Olmsted Brothers to create a design for the park. Negotiations with the city and nearby landowners dragged on, but the property was finally transferred to the city in 1931. Existing mansions were demolished, new roads and pathways laid out, walls and bridges erected, lawns and playgrounds constructed, and mature trees brought in to transform 56 formerly private acres into one of New York's most beautiful amenities. In 1935 **Fort Tryon Park**, constructed entirely at Rockefeller's expense, officially opened to the public.

Fort Tryon Park is one of the very best places along the river from which to gaze across the Hudson to the majestic Palisades. The distinctive 20-mile-long line of basalt cliffs has been admired as a scenic phenomenon since the first explorers ventured up the Hudson, but by the 1880s aggressive quarrying was causing serious damage. Distressed, the New Jersey Federation of Women's Clubs took the lead in pressing for government action to preserve the scenic cliffs, and in 1900 Governors Theodore Roosevelt of New York and Foster Voorhees of New Jersey jointly signed a bill creating the **Palisades Interstate Park Commission**.

Banker George Perkins, whose estate lay across the river in the Bronx, led efforts to supplement public appropriations with private contributions from J. P. Morgan and John D. Rockefeller to acquire land for the new park. Rockefeller, eager to secure the view across the river from Fort Tryon Park, made an additional sizable gift of land in 1933 and pressed for the

Figure 8.10. View of the Palisades.

creation of a clifftop parkway. Construction began in 1947 and was completed in 1958. Today Palisades Interstate Park stretches a full 12 miles from just below the George Washington Bridge to just north of the New York/New Jersey state line.

While negotiations surrounding the creation of Fort Tryon Park were underway, Rockefeller was also working closely with the Metropolitan Museum of Art to acquire the remarkable collection of the eccentric American sculptor George Gray Barnard. During his years living in France Barnard had amassed formidable holdings of medieval sculpture, which he housed in a reproduction cloister on the heights just outside Rockefeller's planned park. In 1925 the philanthropist underwrote the purchase of Barnard's holdings for the Metropolitan. He subsequently also agreed to build in the park, at his own expense, a new museum to house the collection. The **Cloisters**, a branch of the Metropolitan, opened in 1938.

The evocative structure, integrating components from four actual medieval cloisters, was designed by Charles Collens, architect of another Rockefeller benefaction, Riverside Church. Today, the museum's picturesque medieval tower is visible for miles, rising above the greenery of the park.

Figure 8.11. The Cloisters.

Just north of the Cloisters, the hills of Fort Tryon Park drop down to another of Manhattan's natural east–west valleys. The path slopes down under the highway and the railroad to Dyckman Street. Named for the family whose eighteenth-century farmhouse stands nearby on Broadway, Dyckman Street runs all the way across Manhattan, connecting the Hudson and Harlem Rivers. The street's western terminus was long known as **Tubby Hook**. Between 1915 and 1942 a popular ferry shuttled passengers from here across the river to the Palisades. Today the former ferry site is home to a city-owned marina and to a popular riverside restaurant. It is here that the path northward rejoins the riverbank.

The route described above, which runs from the George Washington Bridge north to Dyckman Street, is direct but has the disadvantage of running directly along the side of the northbound lane of the Henry Hudson Parkway. For those hoping for a more tranquil experience, there is an alternative.

Just after climbing the hill north of the George Washington Bridge, watch for an overpass crossing the Henry Hudson Parkway. Take the bridge, and on the far side turn south for half a block to West 181st Street. Follow 181st Street up the hill to Cabrini Boulevard and turn left. You will soon pass between the buildings of Castle Village on your left and those of Hudson View Gardens on the right. Cabrini Boulevard will eventually lead you past the Cabrini Shrine to Margaret Corbin Circle at the entrance to Fort Tryon Park. Walk into the park and through the celebrated Heather Garden to the beautiful Linden Terrace. From there follow signs to the Cloisters. Just north of the museum the path descends through the park to Riverside Drive and Dyckman Street. At Dyckman, head westward toward the river.

Just to the north of Dyckman Street the land rises again, this time into densely wooded **Inwood Hill Park**. In contrast to the city's other parks, Inwood Hill is largely undeveloped and incorporates at its heart the only remaining stand of virgin forest in Manhattan. Hidden among the trees are a series of caves and the ruins of a Revolutionary War fort. The park remains perhaps the only place in Manhattan to experience something of how the island looked before development. There are real woods here, and although the many paths are mostly paved and marked, it can be easy to lose one's way.

In the nineteenth century, Inwood Hill, like what is now Fort Tryon Park to the south, was a popular spot for country houses. These were gradually replaced by a collection of asylums and institutions. In 1895

Andrew Haswell Green, who did so much for New York's park system, began advocating for the conversion of Inwood Hill into a public park. Beginning around 1915 the city slowly acquired the parcels of land that today make up the 196-acre park. Inwood Hill Park officially opened in 1926 with a ceremony including representatives from the indigenous tribes that once lived and hunted here. Additional major work in the park took place during the Depression. Walking paths were laid and the remains of old homes and institutions demolished, leaving the park in its current wilderness state. At the same time, a major landfill project created additional space for recreational facilities along the bank of the river. This is the site of the Inwood ball fields and the route of the riverside path.

From Dyckman Street, follow the path along the west side of the river-level ball fields. There are pleasing views here across the Hudson to the Englewood marina opposite. To the south on the cliffs above the marina is **St. Michael's Villa**, an infirmary and residence operated by the Sisters of St. Joseph of Peace.

Just past the ball fields, the path veers to the east leading to the steps of a metal bridge over the railway. On the far side the route continues north, winding through the woods to the northern end of Inwood Hill Park and an impressive overlook. Just below is the **Spuyten Duyvil Railway Bridge**, originally opened in 1848 by the New York and Hudson River Railroad to provide passenger and freight service down the west side of Manhattan.

When the Hudson River Railroad became a part of the New York Central system in 1869, passenger service was diverted along Harlem River to enter Manhattan across a bridge at 134th Street before proceeding down Park Avenue to Grand Central Terminal. Freight traffic continued to use the

Figure 8.12. Spuyten Duyvil Railway Bridge.

Hudson River Railroad tracks. Today a newer swing bridge, constructed in 1900, carries Amtrak Empire Service trains from Penn Station to Albany and stations along the river. From the overlook above the railroad bridge there are fine views north up the Hudson to the Tappan Zee.

Directly ahead, the looming span of the **Henry Hudson Bridge** marks the northern tip of Manhattan Island.

The handsome arched bridge opened in 1936 as the final link in Robert Moses's plan for an arterial highway running the length of Manhattan Island along the Hudson shore. The bridge, designed by David Steinman, carries the Henry Hudson Parkway northward to connect with the Sawmill Parkway in the Bronx.

Both the road and railway bridges span **Spuyten Duyvil** creek. The Dutch name, literally "spinning devil," is generally thought to refer to the swirling conditions in the creek where the waters of the Hudson and Harlem Rivers meet. The Lenape, who were active here, had a more relaxing name for the creek: Shorakapok, "the sitting down place." In fact, until 1895 the creek was little more than a narrow, winding stream. It was virtually unnavigable and so shallow that it barely served to make Manhattan an island. Proposals to open shipping access between the Hudson and Long Island Sound via the Harlem River were considered as early as 1829, but it was not until 1888 that work to deepen and straighten the creek began. In the

Figure 8.13. Henry Hudson Bridge.

process of creating the new channel, the neighborhood of Marble Hill, for centuries a physical part of Manhattan, was lopped off and marooned in the Bronx. Although no longer connected to the island, it is still a legal part of the borough of Manhattan. At the time of the road bridge's construction in 1936, additional widening and straightening work was undertaken on what became known as the **Harlem Ship Canal**.

We have reached our goal, the northern tip of Manhattan. Where to go now? Perhaps the best way to conclude the walk is to continue along the path under the Henry Hudson Bridge, descending along an attractive trail overlooking the Muscota Marsh to the ball fields on the northern edge of Inwood Hill Park. From there it is an easy few blocks walk east to Broadway, where one can catch a bus or connect with the No. 1 subway train at 215th Street. They will carry you back downtown.

Bibliography

Adams, Arthur G., and Raymond J. Baxter. *Railroad Ferries of the Hudson*. Fordham University Press, 1999.
Adams, Arthur. *The Hudson River Guidebook*. Fordham University Press, 1996.
Adler, Cy A. *Walking Manhattan's Rim, The Great Saunter*. Green Eagle Press, 2003.
Alpern, Andrew. *Apartments for the Affluent*. McGraw-Hill, 1975.
Alpern, Andrew. *Luxury Apartment Houses of Manhattan*. Dover, 1992.
Azzarone, Stephanie. *Heaven on the Hudson: Mansions, Marvels, and Monuments of Riverside Park*. Empire State Editions, 2022.
Boone, Kevin. *The New York Waterfront*. n.d.
Boyle, Robert. *The Hudson River: A Natural and Unnatural History*. Norton, 1969.
Burroughs, Edwin G., and Mike Wallace. *Gotham: A History of New York to 1898*. Oxford University Press, 2000.
Buttenwieser, Ann. *Manhattan Water-Bound*. Syracuse University Press, 1999.
Condit, Carl. *The Port of New York*. 2 vols. University of Chicago Press, 1981.
Doig, Jameson. *Empire on the Hudson: Entrepreneurial Vision and Political Power at the Port of New York Authority*. Columbia University Press, 2001.
Dolkart, Andrew S. *Morningside Heights, A History of Its Architecture and Development*. Columbia University Press, 1998.
Dunwell, Frances F. *The Hudson: America's River*. Columbia University Press, 2008.
Federal Writers Project. *New York City Guide*, 1939. Repr., *The WPA Guide to New York City*. Pantheon Books, 1982.
Gastil, Raymond W. *Beyond the Edge: New York's New Waterfront*. Princeton Architectural Press, 2002.
Grimm, Edward. *Riverside Park: The Splendid Sliver*. Columbia University Press, 2007.
Jackson, Kenneth T., ed. *The Encyclopedia of New York City*. Yale University Press, 1995.
Kellerman, Regina. *The Architecture of the Greenwich Village Waterfront*. New York University Press, 1989.

Koeppel, Gerard. *City of a Grid: How New York Became New York.* Da Capo Press, 2015.
Landau, Sarah Bradford. "The Row Houses of New York's West End." *Journal of the Society of Architectural Historians* 34 (March 1975): 19–36.
Levine, David. *The Hudson Valley: The First 250 Million Years.* Globe Pequot, 2020.
Lopate, Phillip. *Waterfront: A Journey Around Manhattan.* Crown Publishers, 2004.
Miller, Tom. *Seeking New York: The Stories Behind the Historic Architecture of Manhattan One Building at a Time.* Rizzoli International Publications, 2015.
Sanderson, Eric W. *Mannahatta, A Natural History of New York City.* Abrams, 2009.
Schlichting, Kurt C. *Waterfront Manhattan: from Henry Hudson to the High Line.* Johns Hopkins University Press, 2018.
Stern, Robert A. M., David Fishman, and Jacob Tilove. *New York 2000: Architecture and Urbanism Between the Bicentennial and the Millennium.* Monacelli Press, 2006.
Stern, Robert A. M., Gregory Gilmartin, and John Montague Massengale. *New York 1900: Metropolitan Architecture and Urbanism 1890–1915.* Rizzoli, 1983.
Stern, Robert A. M., Gregory Gilmartin, and Thomas Mellins. *New York 1930: Architecture and Urbanism Between the Two World Wars.* Rizzoli, 1987.
Stern, Robert A. M., Thomas Mellins, and David Fishman. *New York 1960: Architecture and Urbanism Between the Second World War and the Bicentennial.* Monacelli Press, 1995.
Stern, Robert A. M., Thomas Mellins, and David Fishman. *New York 1880: Architecture and Urbanism in the Gilded Age.* Monacelli Press, 1999.
True, Clarence. *Riverside Drive.* Press of Unz, 1899.
Wakin, Daniel J. *The Man with the Sawed Off Leg and Other Tales of a New York City Block.* Arcade Publishing, 2018.
Wallace, Mike. *Greater Gotham: A History of New York City from 1898 to 1919.* Oxford University Press, 2017.
White, Norval. *New York: A Physical History.* Atheneum, 1987.
White, Norval, Elliot Willensky, and Fran Leadon. *AIA Guide to New York City.* 5th ed. Oxford University Press, 2010.
Writers Program, Works Projects Administration for the City of New York. *A Maritime History of New York.* Doubleday, Doran, 1941.

Further Information

Helpful electronic resources include the official New York City landmark and historic district designation reports (https://www1.nyc.gov/site/lpc/designations/designation-reports.page). Tom Miller's website "A Daytonian in Manhattan" is a fascinating source for information on individual buildings (http://daytoninmanhattan.blogspot.com/), and both the Bowery Boys website (https://www.boweryboyshistory.com/) and Christopher Gray's long-running Streetscapes columns in *The New York Times* are packed with information and insights. A website devoted to walking Riverside Drive (https://ajs55.wordpress.com/?s=Riverside+Drive&submit=Search) is also helpful, as are the excellent websites maintained by Battery Park City, Hudson River Park, Riverside Park, and the NYC Department of Parks. There are countless online resources devoted to the Hudson River itself.

www.ingramcontent.com/pod-product-compliance
Lightning Source LLC
Chambersburg PA
CBHW050635160426
43194CB00010B/1681